KÖNEMANN

© 2016 koenemann.com GmbH
www. koenemann.com

Editorial project:

booq publishing, S.L.
c/ València, 93, Pral. 1ª
08029 Barcelona, Spain

Editorial coordinator: Claudia Martínez Alonso
Art director: Mireia Casanovas Soley
Edition and texts: Manel Gutiérrez (@mgutico)
Layout: Cristina Simó Perales
Translations: Thinking Abroad

ISBN 978-3-95588-182-5]

Printed in Spain

"A house is a machine for living in. (...) A house must be the case in life, happiness machine". Undoubtedly, this remains one of the most famous, repeated and valid of Le Corbusier's quotes.

The contemporary home has far exceeded the challenges that were already posed at the beginning of last century. In an optimal and rational way, architecture has succeeded in solving all the technical, functional and economic challenges associated with housing design, while at the same time meeting the daily living needs of modern man.

Taking a functional view of architecture, a house perfectly fulfils its purpose: to provide shelter and protection, to be a refuge and a home for its occupants. A home in service of human life, where beauty and design are subordinate to the primary necessities that are imposed upon it by human beings.

But happiness does not only come by way of the functional, nor solely from serving its inhabitants. Inevitably, beauty and design have ceased to be an obstacle in architecture. If a house is to bring happiness, it needs to be beautiful. Beauty is non-negotiable, and architecture has succeeded. A home is a place in which to live but also a place of beauty and, therefore, a place that emanates happiness.

In this book, you will find some of the most beautiful and spectacular homes of today. Beautiful and flamboyant in their original and innovative designs and in their solutions to myriad architectural challenges. But beautiful also because in each there is something fundamental: the measure of its design is always the measure of man.

"Ein Haus ist eine Maschine zum Wohnen. (...) Das Haus muss ein Alleskönner sein, ein Tausendsassa, die Glücksmaschine". Dies ist und bleibt unleugbar einer der berühmtesten, am häufigsten wiederholten und gültigsten Sätze von Le Corbusier.

Das moderne Wohnhaus hat die Herausforderungen, die sich bereits Anfang des vergangenen Jahrhunderts stellten, längst überwunden. Der Architektur ist es auf optimale und rationale Weise gelungen, die ganze Reihe technischer, funktionaler und wirtschaftlicher Herausforderungen zu lösen, die mit dem Entwurf eines Hauses zusammenhängen; und befriedigt zugleich die täglichen Wohnbedürfnisse des modernen Menschen.

In einer funktionalen Vision der Architektur erfüllt das Haus sein Ziel perfekt: Es bietet Zuflucht und Schutz, ist Rückzugsort und Lebensraum für die Menschen. Das Haus im Dienste des menschlichen Lebens. Wo sich Schönheit und Design den Bedingungen untergeordnet finden, die menschliches Tun als oberste Notwendigkeit auferlegt.

Dennoch kommt das Glück nicht allein durch die Funktionalität, nicht nur aus dem Dienste am Menschen. Schönheit und Design sind zwangsläufig kein Hindernis mehr für die Architektur. Wenn ein Haus glücklich machen soll, muss es schön sein. Die Schönheit ist nicht verhandelbar. Und die Architektur hat dies erreicht. Das Haus ist ein Ort zum Wohnen, aber auch ein schöner Ort und demzufolge ein Ort, aus dem Glück hervorgeht.

In diesem Buch können Sie einige der schönsten und spektakulärsten Häuser unserer Zeit finden. Schönes und Spektakuläres in den originellen und innovativen Designs, in den Lösungen für vielfältige architektonische Herausforderungen. Aber auch Schönheit, weil etwas Grundlegendes nach wie vor klar ist: Die Größe des Designs ist immer die Größe des Menschen.

"Une maison est une machine à habiter. (...)La maison doit être le cas dans la vie, machine à bonheur". Indéniablement, cette phrase reste l'une des phrases les plus célèbres, les plus répétées et les plus actuelles de Le Corbusier.

La maison contemporaine a de loin dépassé les défis déjà posés au début du siècle passé. L'architecture, de manière optimale et rationnelle, a réussi à résoudre toute la série de défis techniques, fonctionnels et économiques liés à la conception d'une maison; tout en répondant aux besoins quotidiens de logement de l'homme moderne.

Dans une perspective fonctionnelle de l'architecture, la maison remplit parfaitement son objectif : être un abri et une protection, être un refuge et un lieu pour les personnes. La propriété au service de la vie humaine, où la beauté et le design se trouvent soumis aux conditions qu'impose un fait humain de première nécessité.

Cependant, le bonheur ne vient pas seulement par le biais de ce qui est fonctionnel, ni par le service qu'il rend aux personnes. Inévitablement, la beauté et le design ont cessé d'être un obstacle pour l'architecture. Si la maison doit apporter du bonheur, la maison doit être belle. La beauté n'est pas négociable. Et l'architecture y est arrivée. La maison est un lieu pour vivre, mais également un lieu magnifique et, par conséquent, un lieu d'où émane le bonheur.

Vous pourrez trouver, dans ce livre, quelques-unes des maisons les plus belles et les plus exceptionnelles qui existent actuellement. Beauté et caractère spectaculaire dans des conceptions originales et innovantes, dans les solutions proposées pour les multiples défis architecturaux. Mais également, beauté parce que pour chacune d'elles il existe une chose essentielle : la mesure de sa conception est toujours à la mesure de l'homme.

'Una casa es una máquina para vivir. (...) La casa debe ser el estuche de la vida, la máquina de felicidad'. Innegablemente, esta sigue siendo una de las frases más famosas, repetidas y vigentes de Le Corbusier.

La vivienda contemporánea ha superado con creces los retos que ya se planteaban a principios del siglo pasado. La arquitectura, de forma óptima y racional, ha logrado solucionar toda la serie de retos técnicos, funcionales y económicos ligados al diseño de la vivienda; satisfaciendo a la vez, las necesidades diarias del habitar del hombre moderno.

En una visión funcional de la arquitectura, la vivienda cumple a la perfección con su objetivo: proporcionar cobijo y protección, ser refugio y habitación para las personas. La vivienda al servicio de la vida humana. Donde belleza y diseño se encuentran subordinados a las condiciones que impone un hecho humano de primera necesidad.

Sin embargo, la felicidad no llega solo por la vía de lo funcional, no solo a partir del servicio a las personas. Inevitablemente, belleza y diseño han dejado de ser un obstáculo para la arquitectura. Si la vivienda ha de proporcionar felicidad, la vivienda ha de ser bella. La belleza es innegociable. Y la arquitectura lo ha logrado. La vivienda es un lugar donde vivir, pero también un lugar bello y, por consiguiente, un lugar de donde emana felicidad.

En esta obra, podrá encontrar algunas de las casas más bellas y espectaculares de nuestros días. Belleza y espectacularidad en los originales e innovadores diseños, en las soluciones a los múltiples retos arquitectónicos. Pero también, belleza porque en todas ellas queda patente algo elemental: las medida de su diseño es siempre la medida del hombre.

SILVERWOODHOUSE

3r Ernesto Pereira
Mindelo, Portugal
© Joao Morgado

Ernesto Pereira's remodelling project transformed a soulless house, with a typically rural interior and exterior layout, into a fascinating place for his clients to live in. The transformation brings the beach closer to the owners, helping them to feel the proximity of the dunes, sand and untreated wood every day.

Le travail de rénovation d'Ernesto Pereira parvient à transformer une maison sans âme, avec une distribution intérieure et extérieure typique d'une interprétation rurale, en une œuvre d'art, en un produit fascinant où les clients se voient y vivre. La transformation a lieu en amenant la plage aux propriétaires, en leur faisant ressentir, chaque jour, la proximité des dunes, du sable et du bois non traité.

Dem Umbau von Ernesto Pereira gelingt es, ein Haus ohne Seele mit einer typisch ländlichen Innen- und Außenaufteilung in ein Kunstwerk zu verwandeln, in ein faszinierendes Werk, in dem die Auftraggeber leben. Diese Verwandlung wurde dadurch erreicht, dass der Strand den Bewohnern näher gebracht wurde, indem sie Tag für Tag die Dünen, den Sand und das unbearbeitete Holz spüren können.

La obra de remodelación de Ernesto Pereira logra transformar una casa sin alma, con una distribución interior y exterior típica de una interpretación rural, en una obra de arte, en un producto fascinante donde los clientes se ven viviendo. La transformación se produce al acercar la playa a los propietarios, al hacer sentir, cada día, la proximidad de las dunas, la arena y la madera no tratada.

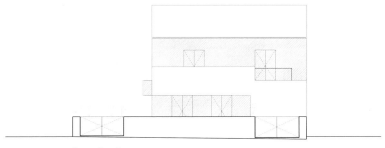

Front elevation

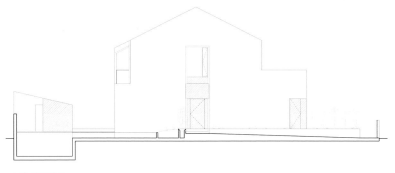

Left elevation

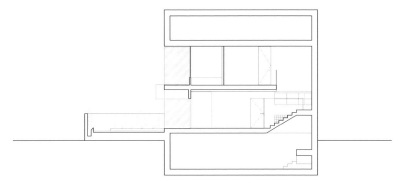

Section A-A

Section B-B

The design develops a strategy of harvesting shapes. Roofs and eaves are used to create multiple open-air spaces.

La conception développe une stratégie de soustraction de volumes. Les toits et les auvents permettent de créer de nombreux espaces en plein air.

Das Design entwickelt eine Strategie zur Reduktion von Volumen. Es werden Dächer und Überstände errichtet, die die Entstehung verschiedenster Räume außen ermöglichen.

El diseño desarrolla una estrategia de sustracción de volúmenes. Se tallan cubiertas y aleros que permiten la creación de múltiples espacios al aire libre.

Second floor plan

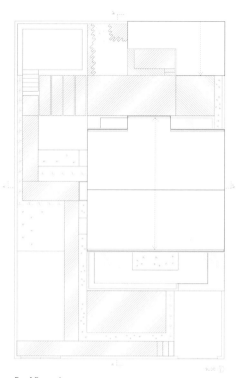

Roof floor plan

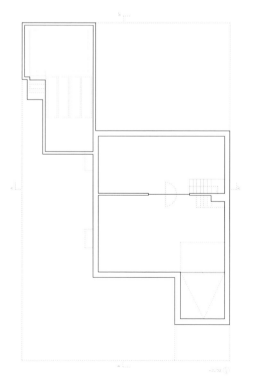

Basement floor plan

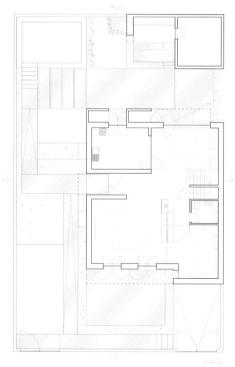

First floor plan

The interior reflects the complexity of the owners' tastes, with made-to-measure accessories designed by the architect himself.

L'intérieur reflète la complexité des goûts des propriétaires, avec des objets faits sur mesure conçus par l'architecte lui-même.

Die Innenräume reflektieren die Komplexität des Geschmacks der Eigentümer, sonderangefertigte Accessoires wurden vom Architekten selbst designt.

El interior refleja la complejidad de los gustos de los propietarios, con accesorios a medida diseñados por el propio arquitecto.

BALIN HOUSE

Fran Silvestre Arquitectos
Bétera, Spain
© Diego Opazo

This Fran Silvestre project is based on elliptical lines that contain the design, maximising the opportunities provided for under regulations and minimising the volumetric impact on the site. This creates a single structure with a continuous façade, which appears to contain only one floor and whose aerodynamic visual nature draws the eye towards the neighbouring landscape.

La conception du projet de Fran Silvestre se dessine autour d'un plan elliptique, qui optimise les possibilités imposées par les normes et qui minimise l'impact volumétrique sur le lieu. Ce qui donne un bâtiment avec une façade continue, qui semble abriter un seul étage et dont l'apparence visuellement aérodynamique transporte le regard sur le paysage alentour.

Das Projekt von Fran Silvestre zeichnet sich durch elliptische Linien aus, die den Entwurf beherrschen, die durch die Vorschriften gegebenen Möglichkeiten maximieren und die volumetrische Auswirkung auf den Ort minimieren. So entsteht eine durchgehende Fassade, die nur ein Stockwerk zu beherbergen scheint und deren optische Aerodynamik den Blick auf die umgebende Landschaft abschweifen lässt.

El proyecto de Fran Silvestre se dibuja a través de trazas elípticas que contienen el diseño, maximizando las posibilidades dadas por la normativa y minimizando el impacto volumétrico sobre el lugar. Se dispone así una pieza con una fachada continua, que parece albergar una sola planta y cuya condición visualmente aerodinámica hace que la mirada se fugue hacia el paisaje vecino.

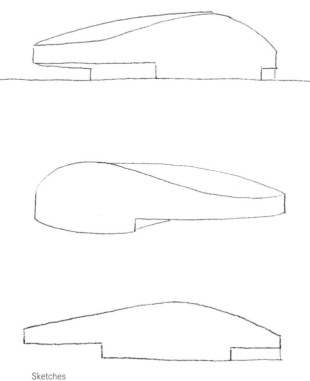

Sketches

The property is positioned to provide the largest possible surface area on the southern edge of the plot for use as a garden.

La maison est construite de façon à laisser la plus grande surface possible du côté sud de la parcelle pour l'utiliser comme jardin.

Das Haus ist auf eine Weise positioniert, dass die größtmögliche Fläche an der Südseite des Grundstücks frei bleibt, um sie als Garten nutzen zu können.

La vivienda se sitúa de forma que se libera la mayor superficie posible en el frente sur de la parcela para aprovecharla como jardín.

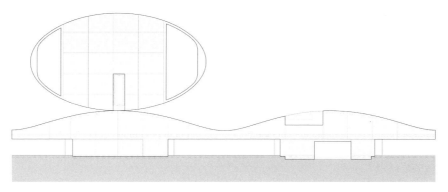

Plan of house skin

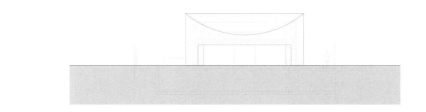

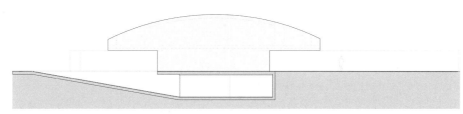

Elevations

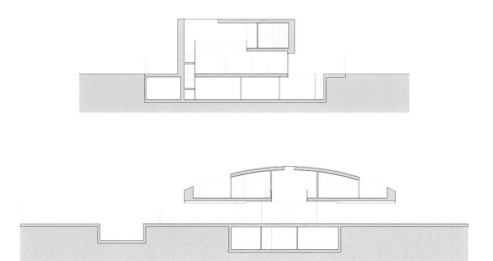

Sections

The interior living space is created around a central space, which acts as the communication hub.

L'espace intérieur de la maison s'articule autour d'un îlot central vide qui est le centre de communication.

Der Innenraum des Hauses artikuliert sich durch ein zentrales Vakuum, in dem sich der Kommunikationskern befindet.

El espacio interior de la vivienda se articula mediante un vacío central en el que se encuentra el núcleo de comunicación.

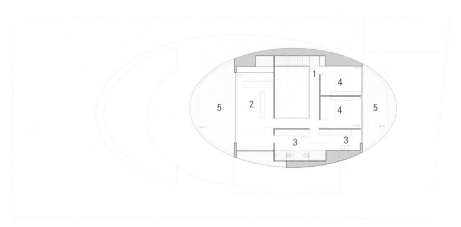

First floor plan

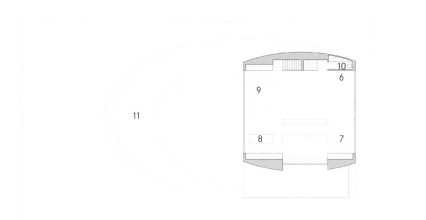

Ground floor plan

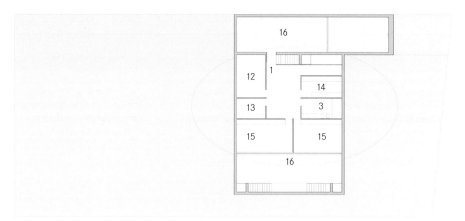

1. Hallway
2. Master bedroom
3. Bathroom
4. Bedroom
5. Terrace
6. Entrance
7. Kitchen
8. Dining room
9. Living room
10. Toilet
11. Swimming pool
12. Mechanical room
13. Wine cellar
14. Laundry
15. Room
16. Parking
17. Patio

Basement floor plan

Service areas, facilities and kitchen convert into right angles the curved lines of the ground floor, which is open to the garden.

Les espaces de service, les installations et la cuisine, permettent de transformer orthogonalement le tracé arrondi du rez-de-chaussée qui s'ouvre sur le jardin.

Die Diensträume, Ausstattung und Küche lassen den kurvigen Verlauf des zum Garten hin offenen unteren Geschosses rechtwinklig werden.

Los espacios de servicio, las instalaciones y la cocina, permiten convertir en ortogonal el trazado curvo de la planta baja abierta al jardín.

THE MIRROR HOUSES

Peter Prichler Architecture
Bolzano, Italy
© Oskar Da Riz, © Nicolò Degiorgis

The client, who also lives on this land in a restored 1960s farmhouse, asked Peter Pichler to design a luxury rental property. The result was two separate apartments in which a family could fully enjoy the experience of living amongst nature, with the maximum degree of privacy between the owner and guests.

Le client, qui vit sur place, dans une maison de campagne restaurée des années 60, a demandé à Peter Pichler de lui concevoir une structure de luxe pour la louer. Le résultat a donné deux appartements autonomes où une famille peut profiter pleinement de l'expérience de vivre au milieu de la nature, tout en préservant l'intimité entre le propriétaire et les hôtes.

Der Auftraggeber, der selbst vor Ort in einem restaurierten Landhaus aus den 60er Jahren lebt, beauftragte Peter Pichler mit dem Entwurf eines Luxusbaus zur Vermietung. Das Ergebnis waren zwei autonome Apartments, wo eine Familie die Erfahrung des Lebens mitten in der Natur voll und ganz genießen kann, mit einem maximalen Grad an Privatsphäre zwischen dem Eigentümer und seinen Gästen.

El cliente, que vive en el mismo lugar, en una casa de campo restaurada de los años 60, pidió a Peter Pichler el diseño de una estructura de lujo para su alquiler. El resultado fueron dos apartamentos autónomos donde una familia puede disfrutar plenamente de la experiencia de vivir en medio de la naturaleza, con un grado máximo de privacidad entre el propietario y los huéspedes.

The new building faces east
and has its own private
garden, separate access and
guest parking.

La nouvelle structure est orientée
à l'est, avec son propre jardin
privé, un accès autonome et un
parking pour les hôtes.

Der Neubau ist nach Osten
ausgerichtet, verfügt über
einen eigenen privaten Garten,
eigenen Zugang und Parkplatz
für die Gäste.

La nueva estructura está
orientada hacia el este, con su
propio jardín privado, acceso
autónomo y aparcamiento para
los huéspedes.

Site plan

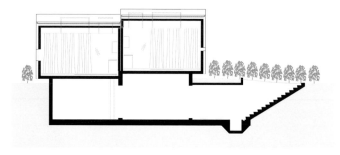

Sections

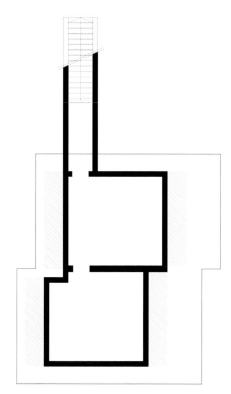

Basement floor plan

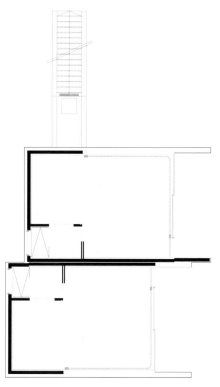

Floor plan

The building opens up to the east with a glass façade, which fades with curved lines into the black aluminium carcass.

Le volume s'ouvre vers l'est grâce à une grande façade en verre, qui s'estompe grâce aux lignes arrondies de la carcasse en aluminium noir.

Der Bau öffnet sich gen Osten mit einer großen Glasfassade, die mit den kurvigen Linien der Karkasse aus schwarzem Aluminium verschwimmt.

El volumen se abre hacia el este en una gran fachada de cristal, que se desvanece con líneas curvas en la carcasa de aluminio negro.

ZAUIA HOUSE

Mario Martins
Vale da Lama, Portugal
© Fernando Guerra [FG+SG]

Paradoxically, this design by Mario Martins Atelier is inspired by the restrictions and limitations of its construction. The result, however, is an architectural work of great simplicity and light, a home characterized by its balanced shapes, precise finish and markedly modern aesthetic.

Paradoxalement, la conception de la maison réalisée par Mario Martins Atelier s'inspire des restrictions et des limites imposées par la construction. Il en résulte, cependant, une maison qui s'entend comme un objet d'architecture, d'une grande simplicité et très lumineuse ; une maison caractérisée par ses formes équilibrées, une finition précise et un caractère clairement moderne.

Paradoxerweise ist der durch Mario Martins Atelier entwickelte Entwurf für dieses Haus durch die Einschränkungen und Begrenzungen der Konstruktion inspiriert. Das Ergebnis ist dennoch ein Wohnhaus, das als architektonisches Objekt verstanden wird, von großer Einfachheit und viel Helligkeit; ein durch seine ausgewogenen Formen, präzises Finish und sein deutlich modernes Wesen charakterisiertes Haus.

Paradójicamente, el diseño de la vivienda realizado por Mario Martins Atelier se inspira en las restricciones y limitaciones impuestas en la construcción. El resultado es, sin embargo, una vivienda entendida como un objeto arquitectónico, de gran simplicidad y mucha luminosidad; una vivienda caracterizada por sus formas equilibradas, su acabado preciso y su carácter marcadamente moderno.

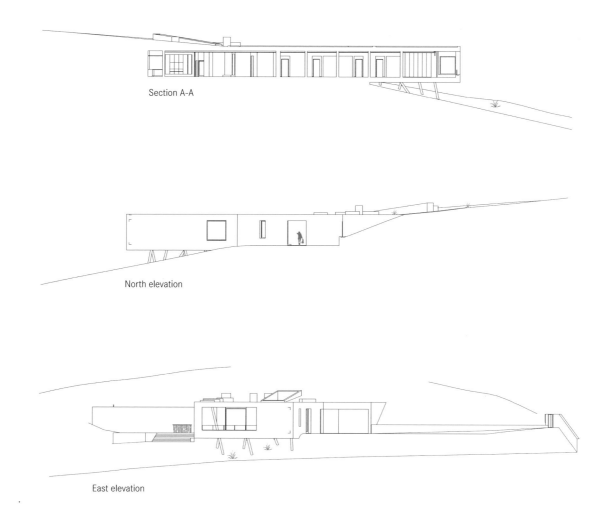

Section A-A

North elevation

East elevation

South elevation

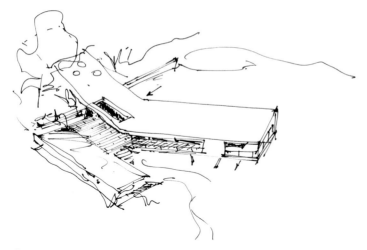
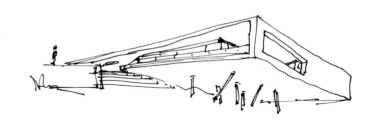

Sketches

Ground floor plan

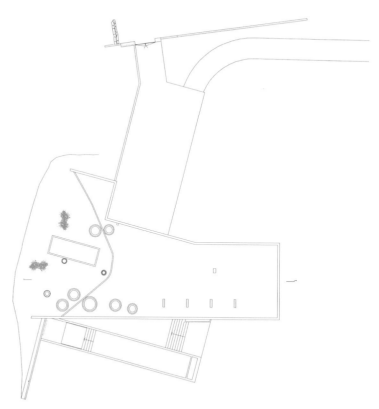

Roof floor plan

Due to the sloping nature of
the terrain, the house is raised
on elegant pillars, reducing the
impact on the natural, indigenous
vegetation that grows beneath it.

En raison de la nature en pente
du terrain, la maison s'élève
sur d'élégants piliers, réduisant
l'impact sur la végétation naturelle
autochtone qui pousse en dessous.

Aufgrund der Hanglage erhebt sich
das Haus auf eleganten Pfeilern,
wodurch die Auswirkungen auf die
autochthone natürliche Vegetation
reduziert werden, die so sogar
unter dem Haus wächst.

Debido a la naturaleza inclinada
del terreno, la vivienda se eleva
sobre elegante pilares, reduciendo
el impacto sobre la vegetación
natural autóctona que crece
debajo de ella.

The office and living room open onto a partially covered patio, which forms part of the front terrace that runs adjacent to all the rooms.

Le bureau et la salle de séjour s'ouvrent sur une large terrasse partiellement couverte, et qui fait partie de la terrasse avant attenante à toutes les pièces.

Arbeits- und Wohnraum öffnen sich zum teilweise überdachten großen Innenhof, der Teil der an alle Zimmer grenzenden vorderen Terrasse ist.

Oficina y sala de estar se abren a un amplio patio parcialmente cubierto, y que forma parte de la terraza delantera contigua a todas las habitaciones.

B+B HOUSE

studio mk27 and galeria arquitetos - marcio kogan
+ renata furlanetto + fernanda neiva
Sao Paulo, Brazil
© Fernando Guerra

The most beautiful and eye-catching element of this project by studio mk27 is the large concrete wall with recesses. The effects created as the light passes through the recesses in the wall are amazing. However, beauty does not stop this original structure from fulfilling its primary function of protecting the interior from the changing weather conditions.

Sans aucun doute, l'élément le plus beau et le plus frappant du projet de studio mk27 est le grand mur formé par des pièces en béton creuses. Les effets créés par la trajectoire de la lumière au travers du mur sont magnifiques et surprenants. Cependant, cette structure originale n'a de cesse de remplir sa fonction première au bénéfice de la beauté : protéger l'intérieur des conditions climatiques changeantes.

Das schönste und auffallendste Element des Projektes von studio mk27 ist zweifelsohne die große Wand aus durchbrochenen Betonsteinen. Die Effekte, die das Licht auf seinem Weg durch die Wand schafft, sind schön und überraschend. Dennoch vernachlässigt die originelle Konstruktion zugunsten der Schönheit nicht ihre Hauptfunktion: Die Innenräume vor den wechselnden klimatischen Bedingungen zu schützen.

Sin duda, el elemento más hermoso y llamativo del proyecto de studio mk27 es la gran pared compuesta de piezas ahuecadas de hormigón. Los efectos que la luz crea en su trayectoria a través de la pared son bellos y sorprendentes. Sin embargo, esta original estructura no deja de cumplir con su función principal en favor de la belleza: proteger el interior de las cambiantes condiciones climáticas.

The long, smooth ramp extends the transition from inside to out, creating the feeling of a constantly changing environment.

La rampe, longue et en pente douce, fait la transition entre l'intérieur et l'extérieur en donnant la sensation constante d'un environnement changeant

Die lange und sanfte Rampe verlängert den Übergang von Innen nach Außen, sie ruft das konstante Gefühl sich verändernder Umgebung hervor.

La rampa, larga y suave, extiende la transición desde el interior al exterior al crear la sensación constante de entorno cambiante.

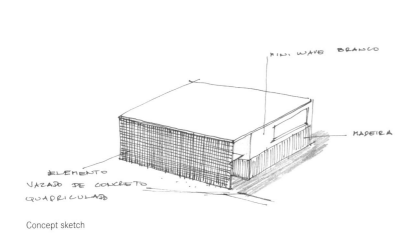

MINI WAVE BRANCO

MADEIRA

ELEMENTO
VAZADO DE CONCRETO
QUADRICULADO

Concept sketch

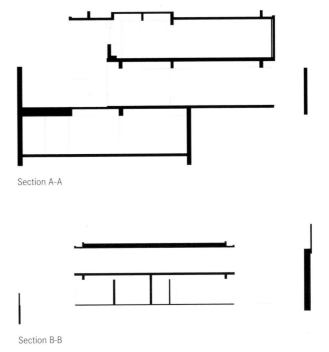

Section A-A

Section B-B

The kitchen counter is located behind the window, which overlooks the ramp. The kitchen is a pleasant space and is well lit by the light that filters in through the hollow spaces.

Le plan de travail de la cuisine se trouve derrière la fenêtre qui donne sur la rampe. La cuisine est un espace agréable et lumineux grâce à la lumière filtrée qu'elle reçoit des éléments creux.

Die Arbeitsplatte in der Küche befindet sich hinter dem Fenster, das zur Rampe hinausgeht. Die Küche ist ein angenehmer und gut beleuchteter Raum, der das durch die durchbrochenen Elemente gefilterte Licht aufnimmt.

La encimera de la cocina se encuentra detrás de la ventana que da a la rampa. La cocina es un espacio agradable y bien iluminado al recibir la luz filtrada por los huecos de la pared.

RIVERBANK

Balance Associates Architects
Big Sky, Montana, United States
© Steve Keating

This project by Balance Associates Architects is located on the banks of the river Gallatin, in an unparalleled natural setting close to Big Sky. The house is designed to create an open and relaxed atmosphere with a strong connection to its exterior surroundings. However, as well as capturing the best views of the river, the two wings create an entrance courtyard that is protected from changes in the weather.

Le projet de Balance Associates Architects se situe le long des rives de la rivière Gallatin, dans un site naturel incomparable près de Big Sky. La maison a été conçue pour créer une atmosphère ouverte, détendue et en lien étroit avec la nature. Cependant, les deux ailes de la maison ne cherchent pas seulement à avoir la plus belle vue sur la rivière mais aussi à avoir une terrasse à l'entrée à l'abri des changements climatiques.

Balance Associates Architects platzieren ihr Projekt ans Ufer des Flusses Gallatin in eine unvergleichliche natürliche Umgebung in der Nähe von Big Sky. Mit dem Entwurf sollte eine offene, entspannte Atmosphäre mit starker Verbindung nach Außen geschaffen werden. Dennoch streben die zwei Flügel des Gebäudes neben dem Einfangen der besten Blicke auf den Fluss danach, einen vor den Wetterwechseln geschützten Eingangshof entstehen zu lassen.

Balance Associates Architects sitúa su proyecto junto a la orilla del río Gallatin, en un paraje natural incomparable cerca de Big Sky. La vivienda se diseñó para crear una atmósfera abierta, relajada y con una fuerte conexión con el exterior. Sin embargo, las dos alas de la casa, además de capturar las mejores vistas del río, buscan crear un patio de entrada protegido de los cambios climáticos.

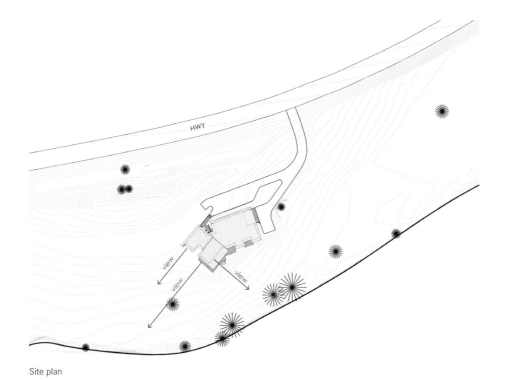

Site plan

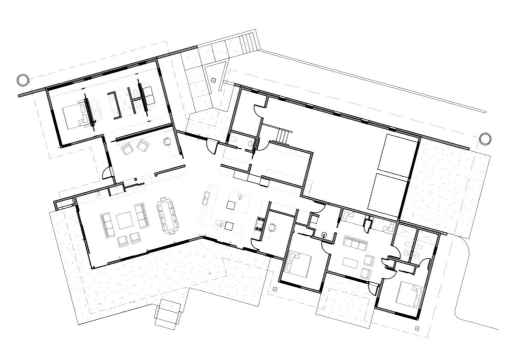

Floor plan

The large roof over the lounge provides shade in summer, while geothermal heat pumps and insulation provide efficient heat in winter.

L'immense toit sur le salon donne de l'ombre en été, tandis que les pompes à chaleur géothermiques et un très bon isolement fournissent une chaleur efficace en hiver.

Das große Dach über dem Salon spendet im Sommer Schatten, während die Erdwärmepumpen und die starke Isolation im Winter auf effiziente Weise Wärme spenden.

El gran techo sobre el salón proporciona sombra en verano, mientras que las bombas de calor geotérmicas y el alto nivel de aislamiento proporcionan calor de forma eficiente en invierno.

The house is divided between the main hall and the guest wing. The guest area can be isolated from the rest of the house and maintained at a lower temperature when it is unoccupied.

La maison est divisée entre le salon principal et l'aile des invités. La partie réservée aux invités peut être isolée du reste de la maison et maintenir une température plus basse lorsqu'elle est inoccupée.

Das Haus ist zwischen dem Hauptsalon und dem Gästeflügel unterteilt. Der Gästebereich kann vom Rest des Hauses abgetrennt werden, wodurch er, wenn er nicht belegt ist, auf niedrigster Temperatur gehalten werden kann.

La casa se divide entre el salón principal y el ala de invitados. La zona de invitados se puede aislar del resto de la vivienda y mantener en ella una temperatura más baja cuando está desocupada.

FLORIDA BEACH HOUSE

iredale pedersen hook architects
Florida Beach, Western Australia, Australia
© Peter Bennetts

This design by iredale pedersen hook architects emphasises the vastness of the nearby Indian Ocean. It is a modern holiday house that sits in contrast to the homes that used to dominate the landscape. The entire space is aligned and extruded through the dialogue between the shape of the footprint and the beautiful undulating cross section, ensuring that we do not forget the intensity and variety of the ocean.

La conception d'iredale pedersen hook architects met l'accent sur la proche immensité de l'océan Indien. C'est une maison de vacances moderne, contrairement aux résidences qui un jour dominèrent le paysage. Tout l'espace de la maison est aligné et extrudé à partir du dialogue entre la forme de l'étage et la jolie ondulation de sa coupe, qui permettent de ne pas oublier l'intensité et le caractère changeant de l'océan.

Der Entwurf von iredale pedersen hook architects betont die nahe Unermesslichkeit des Indischen Ozeans. Es ist ein modernes Ferienhaus im Kontrast zu den Wohnhäusern, die einst die Landschaft dominierten. In ihm richtet und drückt sich der gesamte Raum vom Dialog zwischen der Form des Geschosses und der schönen Wellenlinie seines Schnitts aus, welche daran hindern, die Intensität und Vielfältigkeit des Ozeans zu vergessen.

El diseño de iredale pedersen hook architects enfatiza la cercana inmensidad del océano Índico. Es una moderna casa de vacaciones, en contraste con las residencias que una vez dominaron el paisaje. En ella, todo el espacio se alinea y se extruye a partir del diálogo entre la forma de la planta y la bella ondulación de su sección, y que impiden olvidar la intensidad y variedad del océano.

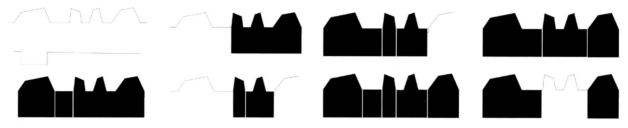

Diagram of sections

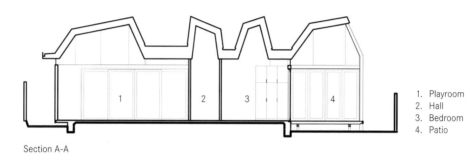

Section A-A

1. Playroom
2. Hall
3. Bedroom
4. Patio

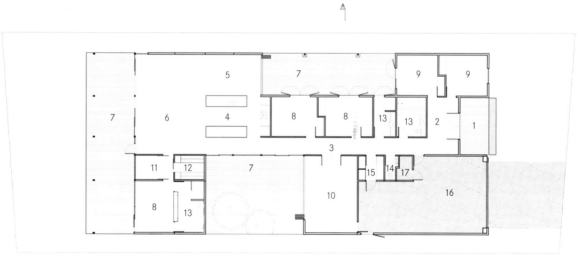

Floor plan

1. Entrance patio
2. Entrance
3. Hall/Gallery
4. Kitchen
5. Dining room
6. Living room
7. Patio
8. Bedroom
9. Guest bedroom
10. Playroom
11. Study
12. Dressing room
13. Bathroom
14. Toilet
15. Laundry
16. Parking
17. Store room

The undulated section, which flows from the beach all the way to the street, stimulates memories of the ocean in the living spaces that do not have direct views of the coast.

La coupe ondulée, de la plage jusqu'à la rue, stimule le souvenir de l'océan dans les espaces de la maison qui n'ont pas de vues directes sur la côte.

Der wellige Schnitt setzt sich vom Strand bis zur Straße fort, er stimuliert die Erinnerung an den Ozean in jenen Räumen des Hauses, die keinen direkten Blick auf die Küste haben.

La sección ondulada, continua desde la playa hasta la calle, estimula el recuerdo del océano en aquellos espacios de la vivienda que no disponen de vistas directas sobre la costa.

Four terraces in each of the cardinal points provide outdoor living for the inhabitants all year round, protected from strong winds and storms.

Quatre terrasses dans chacun des points cardinaux permettent aux occupants de vivre à l'extérieur, en toute saison, à l'abri des vents violents et des orages.

Vier Terrassen, eine in jeder Himmelsrichtung, ermöglichen den Bewohnern ein Leben draußen, geschützt vor den starken Winden und Unwettern der Region, zu jeder Jahreszeit.

Cuatro terrazas en cada uno de los puntos cardinales permiten a los ocupantes vivir en el exterior, protegidos de los fuertes vientos y tormentas del lugar, durante cualquier época del año.

S CUBE CHALET

AGi Architects
Kuwait City, Kuwait
© Nelson Garrido

This property is composed of three intertwined beach houses. The owners, two brothers and sister, each with their own families, wanted to continue to enjoy the exceptional environment in which they grew up, but with independence and privacy. AGi's design is done in duplicate—it retains both privacy and the benefits of the outdoor areas with the terraces.

La propriété est formée de trois maisons de plage entrelacées. Les propriétaires – deux frères et leur sœur, chacun d'eux avec sa propre famille –, souhaitaient continuer à profiter de l'environnement exceptionnel dans lequel ils ont grandi, tout en conservant leur indépendance et leur intimité. Les architectes d'AGi conçoivent la maison selon deux critères : conserver à la fois l'intimité et les avantages des espaces extérieurs grâce aux terrasses.

Das Gebäude besteht aus drei miteinander verbundenen Strandhäusern. Die Eigentümer – zwei Brüder und eine Schwester, alle mit eigener Familie – wollten weiterhin die außergewöhnliche Umgebung genießen, in der sie aufgewachsen sind, jedoch in Unabhängigkeit und Privatsphäre. Der Entwurf von AGi erreicht beides: Er erhält zugleich die Privatsphäre und durch die Terrassen können die Vorteile der Außenbereiche weiter genutzt werden.

La vivienda la componen tres casas de playa entrelazadas. Los propietarios –dos hermanos y su hermana, cada uno con sus propias familias–, querían seguir disfrutando del entorno excepcional en el que crecieron, pero con independencia y privacidad. El diseño de AGi se realiza por duplicado: mantiene a la vez privacidad y los beneficios de las zonas al aire libre mediante las terrazas.

The design of the three intertwined houses creates outdoor spaces that capture the breeze, improving the flow of cool air within the courtyards.

Der Entwurf der drei miteinander verbundenen Häuser schafft Räume an der frischen Luft, die die dominanten Winde einfangen und die Zirkulation innerhalb der Innenhöfe verbessern.

La conception des trois maisons entrelacées crée des espaces extérieurs qui recueillent les vents dominants et améliorent leur passage dans les terrasses.

El diseño de las tres casas entrelazadas crea espacios al aire libre que recogen los vientos dominantes y mejoran su circulación dentro de los patios.

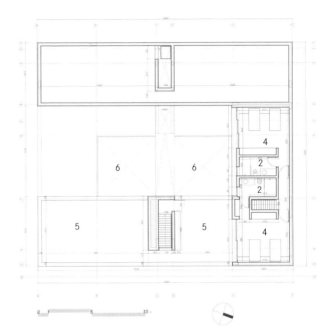

Second floor plan

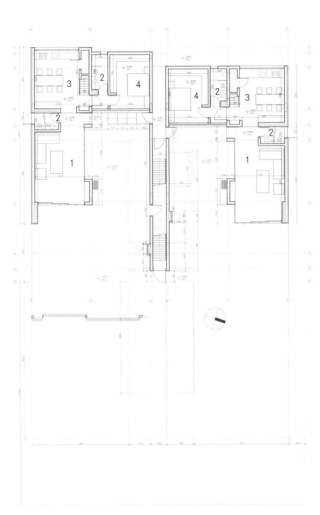

Ground floor plan

1. Living room
2. Bathroom
3. Kitchen
4. Bedroom
5. Terrace
6. Void

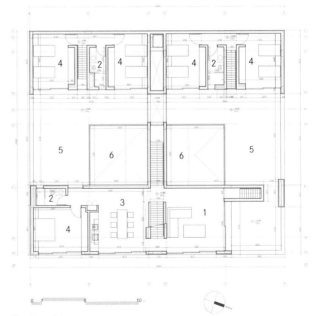

First floor plan

The interiors were designed by AGi, and all the materials used in the project were manufactured locally.

Les intérieurs ont été conçus par les architectes d'AGi, et tous les matériaux utilisés dans le projet ont été fabriqués localement.

Die Innenräume wurden durch die Architekten von AGi gestaltet und alle in diesem Projekt verwendeten Materialien wurden regional hergestellt.

Los interiores han sido diseñados por los arquitectos de AGi, y todos los materiales utilizados en el proyecto han sido fabricados localmente.

EDGE HOUSE

Mobius Architects, Przemek Olczyk
Cracow, Poland
© Pawel Ulatowski

The apartment's original design owes itself to a local anomaly: a sloping plot divided into two levels by a large limestone rock. The lower level gives its owners complete privacy while the upper level provides panoramic views. The result is the expression of the seemingly impossible: getting the most out of both sections of a plot divided by a natural barrier.

La conception originale de la maison est due à une anomalie locale : un terrain en pente coupé par une grande roche calcaire qui sépare la parcelle en deux niveaux. Le niveau inférieur permet aux propriétaires d'avoir une intimité totale, et le niveau supérieur, d'avoir des vues panoramiques. Le résultat paraissait impossible : tirer le meilleur parti des deux niveaux d'une maison divisée par une limite naturelle.

Das originelle Design des Hauses ist einer Anomalie des Ortes geschuldet: Das schräge Grundstück wird durch einen großen Kalksteinfelsen unterbrochen, der es in zwei Ebenen unterteilt. Die untere Ebene mit ungestörter Privatsphäre für die Bewohner und die obere mit Panoramablick. Das Ergebnis ist der Ausdruck dessen, was unmöglich schien: Das Maximum aus den zwei Teilen eines durch eine natürliche Grenze geteilten Hauses herauszuholen.

El original diseño de la vivienda se debe a una anomalía local: un terreno en pendiente cortado por una gran roca caliza que divide la parcela en dos niveles. El inferior, con privacidad total para los propietarios, y el superior, con vistas panorámicas. El resultado es la expresión de lo que parecía imposible: sacar el máximo partido a las dos piezas de una vivienda dividida por un límite natural.

The shape of the house's two wings is softened by wavy wood-clad walls and a green roof to blend in with the environment.

La forme des deux ailes de la maison est adoucie par des murs ondulés recouverts de bois et un toit vert pour se fondre dans l'environnement.

Die Form der zwei Flügel des Hauses wird durch wellenförmige mit Holz verkleidete Wände und ein grünes Dach weicher, um sich besser in die Umgebung einzufügen.

La forma de las dos alas de la vivienda se suaviza con paredes onduladas forradas en madera y un techo verde para mezclarse con el entorno.

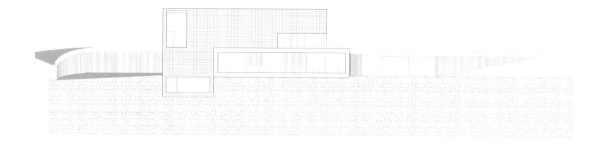

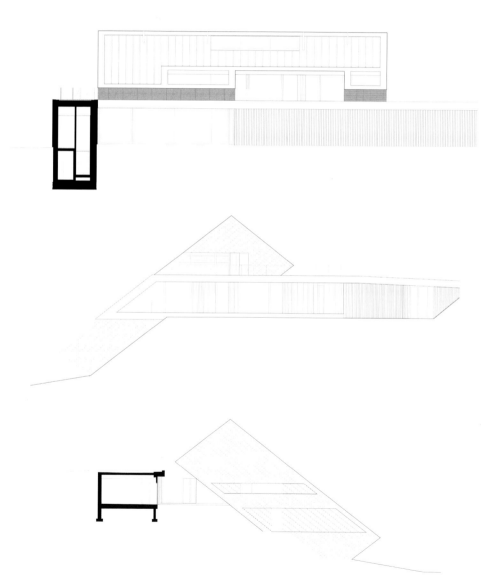

Elevations

The inclined walls form part of the pitched roofs, enabling the house to comply with building regulations —37-degree roofs with eaves.

Les murs inclinés font partie des toits à double pente et permettent de respecter les normes légales de conception — des toits avec des auvents et une inclinaison de 37 degrés.

Die geneigten Wände sind Teil der zweiseitigen Dachhaut und erlauben die Einhaltung der gesetzlichen Anforderungen ans Design — Dächer mit Vordächern und Gefällen von 37 Grad.

Las paredes inclinadas forman parte de las cubiertas a dos aguas y permiten cumplir con los requisitos legales de diseño — tejados con aleros y pendientes de 37 grados.

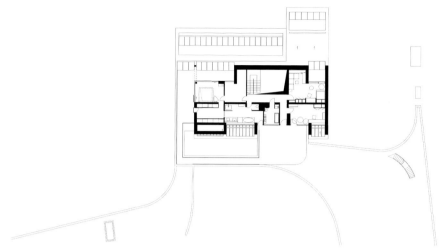

First floor plan

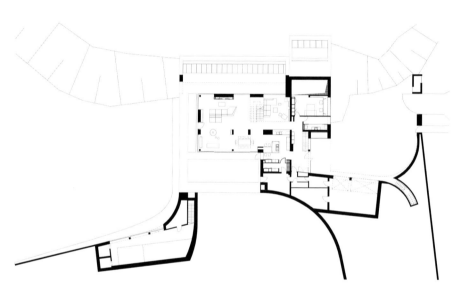

Ground floor plan

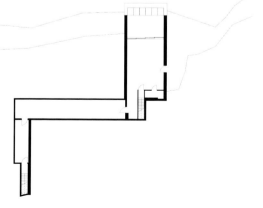

Basement floor plan

V-LODGE

Reiulf Ramstad Arkitekter
Ål, Norway
© Reiulf Ramstad Arkitekter

This chalet is perfect for a family of five all year round. Its design will accommodate changes to the family composition and the mix of future generations. The chalet sits lightly on the gentle slope. Its shape creates little areas with their own microclimate, easily accessible from inside, in which the conditions are perfect for outdoor activities.

Cette cabane est idéale durant toute l'année pour une famille de cinq personnes. En outre, sa conception permettra de s'adapter à n'importe quel changement dans la composition familiale et au mélange des générations futures. La cabane se situe délicatement sur une petite pente; son volume crée de petits microclimats, facilement accessible de l'intérieur, et où les conditions climatiques sont idéales pour les activités en plein air.

Dieses Haus zur ganzjährigen Nutzung ist perfekt für eine Familie mit fünf Personen. Zudem erlaubt sein Design, auf künftige Veränderungen in der Familienstruktur und mehrere Generationen zu reagieren. Das Haus sitzt sanft auf einem leichten Hang; sein Volumen schafft kleine leicht von innen zugängliche Mikroklimas, wo die Sonnenbedingungen geeignet für Aktivitäten an der frischen Luft sind.

Esta cabaña para todo el año es perfecta para una familia de cinco personas. Además, su diseño permitirá dar cabida a cambios en la composición de la familia y a la mezcla de generaciones futuras. La cabaña se asienta suavemente sobre la ligera pendiente; su volumen crea pequeños microclimas, de fácil acceso desde el interior, donde las condiciones solares son idóneas para las actividades al aire libre.

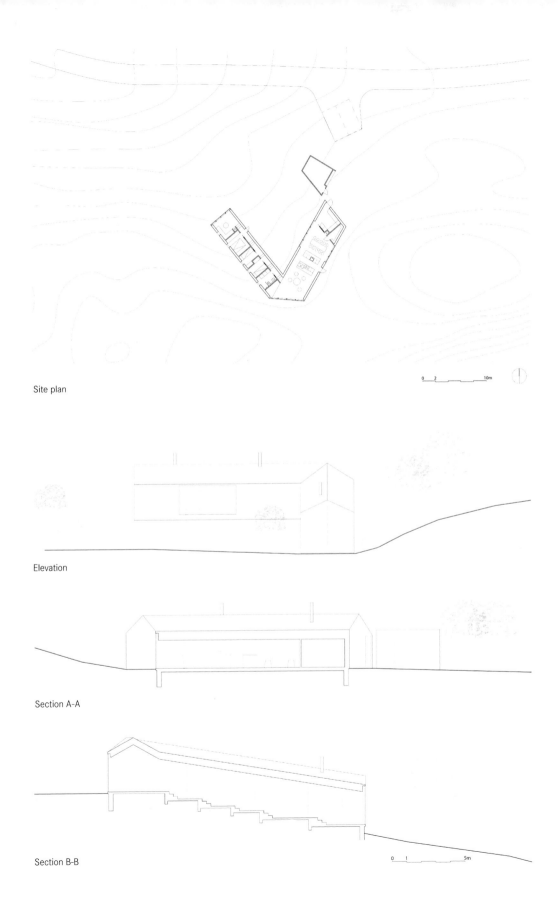

Site plan

0 2   10m

Elevation

Section A-A

Section B-B

0   1   5m

The building comprises two flat shapes joined in a V, with the south-facing wall featuring a large window at the intersection of the chamfer.

Le bâtiment est formé de deux parties unies suivant un plan en forme de V, avec un mur orienté sud et une large baie vitrée à l'intersection du coin.

Das Gebäude besteht aus zwei in Form eines V verbundenen Teilen, die nach Süden ausgerichtete Wand ist an der Schnittstelle der Walmfläche großflächig verglast.

El edificio lo componen dos cuerpos unidos en un plano con forma de V, con la pared orientada al sur con un amplio acristalamiento en la intersección del chaflán.

Outside, the walls and sloping ceilings are clad in heart of pine, providing a smooth skin and integrating perfectly with the surroundings.

À l'extérieur, les murs et les toits inclinés sont recouverts de bois en pin massif, qui donnent un aspect homogène et parfaitement intégré à l'environnement.

Außen sind Mauern und geneigte Dächer mit Kiefernkernholz verkleidet, wodurch eine homogene und perfekt in die Umgebung integrierte Außenhaut entsteht.

En el exterior, muros y techos inclinados están revestidos de madera de corazón de pino, proporcionando una piel homogénea y perfectamente integrada en el entorno.

OUTSIDE IN

Takeshi Hosaka
Yamanashi, Japan
© KOJI FUJII / Nacasa&Partners Inc.

The sky above the house, the forest nearby and the ground below: the natural surroundings are so attractive they are adopted by the interior. Nature is incorporated horizontally and vertically, becoming an integral part of the design of the structure and creating a complete graduation from the outdoor space to the internal areas of the house.

Le ciel au-dessus de la maison, la forêt proche et le sol en dessous : la nature est suffisamment attrayante pour être possédée de l'intérieur. La nature s'intègre à l'horizontale et à la verticale, devient une partie entière de la conception de la structure et crée un changement complet de la partie extérieure aux parties internes de la maison.

Der Himmel über dem Haus, der Wald in der Nähe und der Boden unter den Füßen: Die Natur ist ausreichend attraktiv um vom Inneren vereinnahmt zu werden. Die Natur fließt horizontal und vertikal ein, sie wird zu einem integralen Bestandteil des Designs des Baus und schafft einen kompletten Übergang vom Außenbereich zu den inneren Bereichen des Hauses.

El cielo encima de la casa, el bosque cerca y el suelo debajo: la naturaleza es lo suficientemente atractiva como para poder ser poseída por el interior. La naturaleza se incorpora en horizontal y en vertical, pasa a ser una parte integral del diseño de la estructura y crea una gradación completa desde la zona exterior a las áreas internas de la vivienda.

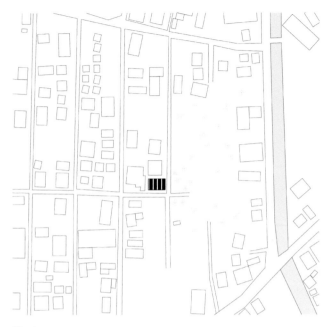

Site plan

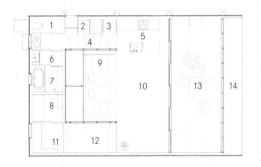

Floor plan

1. Restroom
2. Wash
3. Fridge
4. Utility room
5. Kitchen
6. Washroom
7. Bathroom
8. Closet
9. Children's room
10. Living room
11. Study
12. Bedroom
13. Dining room
14. Porch

The roof of the house is a combination of V-beams of reinforced concrete and clear acrylic that allows its residents to see the sky through the roof.

Le toit de la maison est une combinaison de poutres-V en béton armé et en acrylique transparent qui permet aux habitants de voir le ciel à travers les interstices.

Die Dachkonstruktion des Hauses ist eine Kombination aus V-Trägern aus Stahlbeton und transparentem Acryl, die es den Bewohnern erlaubt, den Himmel durch das Dach zu sehen.

La cubierta de la casa es una combinación de vigas-V de hormigón armado y acrílico transparente que permite que los residentes puedan ver el cielo a través del techo.

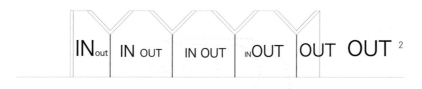

1

IN_{out} IN out IN OUT inOUT OUT OUT ²

3

Concept sketch

1. Sky
2. Forset
3. Ground

Section

1. Roof: Photocatalyst
   Top coat (grey)
   FRP waterproofing
   Plywood t= 12 mm
   Plywood t= 12 mm
   Foaming urethane
   t= 45 mm
2. Toplight: Photocatalyst
   Acrylic board
   (transparence) t= 20 mm
3. Wall: Exposed concrete
   finish
4. Floor: Plastic seat
   (white) t= 2 mm
   Floor heater t= 12 mm
   Plywood t= 12 mm
   Plywood t= 18 mm
   Foaming urethane
   t= 60 mm
5. Ceiling: Exposed
   concrete finish
6. Wall basswood board
   t= 12 mm dyeing
   painting foaming
   urethane t= 25 mm

7. Floor: Walnut flooring
   t= 15 mm
   Floor heater t= 12 mm
   Plywood t= 18 mm
   Foaming urethane
   t= 60 mm
8. Wooden sash (sliding
   door) double glazing
9. Floor: Carpet t= 7 mm
   Plywood t= 9 mm
   Floor heater t= 12 mm
   Foaming urethane
   t= 60 mm
10. Wooden sash (folding
    door) double glazing
11. Clover soil
12. Soil mortar
13. Outdoor facility:
    Gravel t= 100 mm

A. Closet
B. Children's room
C. Living room
D. Dining room

1. Roof: Photocatalyst
            Top coat (grey)
            FRP waterproofing
            Plywood t= 12 mm
            Plywood t= 12 mm
            Foaming urethane t= 45 mm
2. Ceiling: Exposed concrete finish
3. Sealing
4. Wooden sash (folding/sliding door) double
   glazing
5. Dining room
6. Outdoor
7. Clover soil
8. Mortar
9. Floor: Carpet t=7mm
            Plywood t=9mm
            Floor heater t=12mm
            Plywood t= 18 mm
            Foaming urethane t= 60 mm
10. Living room

Folding door section

Sliding door section

GREENFIELD LIVING

MINARC, Erla Dögg Ingjaldsdóttir and Tryggvi Thorsteinsson
Los Angeles, California, United States
© MINARC

'Build us a comfortable, open and modern home where we can watch the children play', was the design brief given to Erla Dögg Ingjaldsdóttir and Tryggvi Thorsteinsson, architects and owners of MINARC, for this private residence. The result reflects the heritage of their home country, Iceland, their love of new materials, sustainability and energy efficiency.

"Créer une maison moderne qui soit confortable et ouverte, d'où nous pourrons voir les enfants jouer", a été l'idée principale qui a guidé la conception de la maison personnelle d'Erla Dögg Ingjaldsdóttir et de Tryggvi Thorsteinsson, architectes et propriétaires de MINARC. Le résultat reflète l'héritage reçu de leur pays d'origine, l'Islande, l'amour pour les matériaux nouveaux, la durabilité et l'efficacité énergétique.

"Ein modernes Haus zu schaffen, das bequem und offen ist, wo wir den Kindern beim Spielen zusehen können", das war die Grundidee, die den Entwurf des Hauses von Erla Dögg Ingjaldsdóttir und Tryggvi Thorsteinsson, Architekten und Inhabern von MINARC, leitete. Das Ergebnis spiegelt das Erbe ihres Heimatlandes Island, die Liebe zu neuen Materialien, Nachhaltigkeit und Energieeffizienz wider.

"Crear una casa moderna que sea cómoda y abierta, donde podamos ver a los niños jugar", esta fue la idea principal que guió el diseño de la vivienda particular de Erla Dögg Ingjaldsdóttir y Tryggvi Thorsteinsson, arquitectos y propietarios de MINARC. El resultado refleja la herencia recibida de su país de origen, Islandia, el amor por los nuevos materiales, la sostenibilidad y la eficiencia energética.

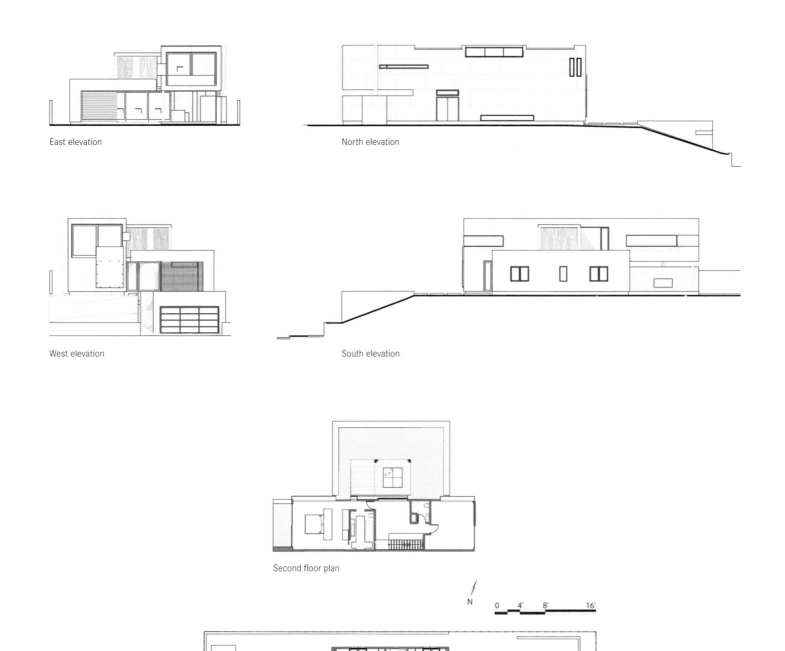

East elevation

North elevation

West elevation

South elevation

Second floor plan

N

0   4'   8'   16'

First floor plan

The large glass doors and windows enable the passage of natural light, meeting the sustainability objectives by reducing energy costs.

Les grandes portes et les baies vitrées permettent à la lumière naturelle de passer et, par conséquent, d'atteindre les objectifs de durabilité en réduisant les dépenses d'énergie électrique.

Die großen Türen und Fensterflächen aus Glas lassen natürliches Licht herein und erfüllen so die Nachhaltigkeitsziele zur Senkung des Energieverbrauchs.

La grandes puertas y ventanales de vidrio permiten el paso de la luz natural y, por tanto, cumplir con los objetivos de sostenibilidad al reducir el gasto de energía eléctrica.

The heart of this house is a practical, open kitchen with a solid orange-surfaced island and an innovative, practical and simple storage system for seven stools.

Le cœur de la maison est une cuisine ouverte, avec un îlot central solide de couleur orange et un système de rangement novateur, pratique et simple pour sept tabourets.

Das Herz des Hauses ist eine offene Küche mit einer Insel mit soliden Oberflächen in Orange und einem innovativen, praktischen und einfachen System zur Aufbewahrung von sieben Hockern.

El corazón de la vivienda es una cocina abierta, con una isla de superficie sólida de color naranja y un innovador, práctico y sencillo sistema de almacenamiento para siete taburetes.

NETTLETON 198

SAOTA - Stefan Antoni Olmesdahl Truen Architects
Cape Town, South Africa
© Adam Letch

Building on an existing structure, the owners wanted to create a six-bedroom house, distributed over seven levels to make the most both of the available space and of the views of sea and mountains. This design by SOATA restructured and remodelled the existing lower levels whilst demolishing the upper one so as to create two additional floors.

Sur une structure qui existait déjà, les propriétaires souhaitaient posséder une maison avec six chambres, repartie sur sept niveaux et utiliser au maximum le terrain disponible ainsi que la vue sur la mer et la montagne. La conception de SAOTA restructure et rénove les niveaux inférieurs préexistants, tout en démolissant le niveau supérieur pour en créer deux nouveaux supplémentaires.

Auf einen bereits vorhandenen Bau wünschten die Eigentümer ein Wohnhaus mit sechs Schlafzimmern, über sieben Ebenen verteilt, sowie die maximale Ausnutzung sowohl des verfügbaren Geländes als auch des Blicks auf Meer und Berge. Das Design von SAOTA restrukturiert und gestaltet die bereits vorhandenen unteren Ebenen um, während die obere Ebene abgerissen wird, um zwei neue zusätzliche Ebenen entstehen zu lassen.

Sobre una estructura preexistente, los propietarios deseaban poseer una vivienda con seis dormitorios, distribuida en siete niveles y para poder aprovechar al máximo tanto el terreno disponible como las vistas al mar y a la montaña. El diseño de SAOTA reestructura y remodela los niveles inferiores preexistentes, mientras que demuele el nivel superior para crear dos niveles adicionales nuevos.

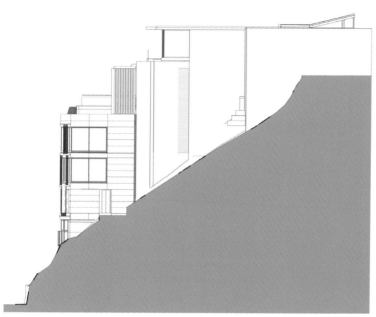

South elevation

West elevation

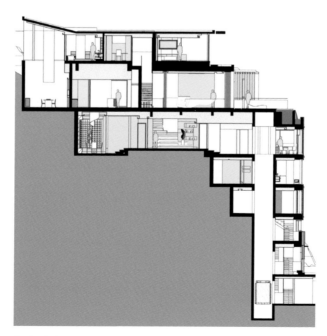

Section A-A

The exterior is clad in powder-painted aluminium, making the finish of the surface robust and precise.

L'extérieur du bâtiment est recouvert de poudre d'aluminium peint, ce qui signifie que la finition superficielle est très solide et précise.

Außen ist das Gebäude mit pulverbeschichtetem Aluminium verkleidet, wodurch ein sehr robustes und präzises Oberflächenfinish entsteht.

El exterior del edificio está revestido de aluminio pintado al polvo, lo cual significa que el acabado superficial es muy robusto y preciso.

The cross ventilation helps to offset the harshness of the sun and the heat. Being open to the east and west creates the sensation of an open pavilion in the living room.

La ventilation transversale aide à compenser le soleil et la chaleur intense. Le salon, entièrement ouvert à l'est et à l'ouest, donne le sentiment d'être un pavillon ouvert.

Die Kreuzventilation trägt dazu bei, die starke Sonneneinstrahlung und die dadurch entstehende Hitze zu kompensieren. Das vollständig nach Osten und Westen offene Wohnzimmer vermittelt das Gefühl, sich in einem offenen Pavillon zu befinden.

La ventilación cruzada ayuda a compensar la dureza del sol y el calor generado. La sala de estar, abierta por completo hacia el este y el oeste, produce la sensación de ser un pabellón abierto.

Sixth floor plan

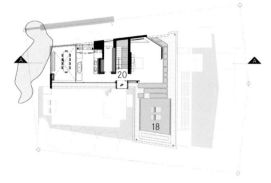

Seventh floor plan

1. Entrance
2. Parking
3. Services
4. Lobby
5. Office
6. Double volume
7. Lounge
8. Kitchen
9. Laundry
10. Yard
11. Bedroom
12. Spa
13. Gym
14. Library
15. Media
16. Wine cellar
17. Bar
18. Terrace
19. Swimming pool
20. Main suite
21. Dining room

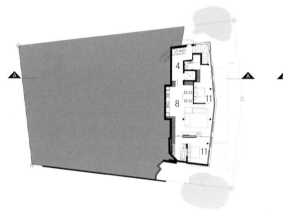

Third floor plan

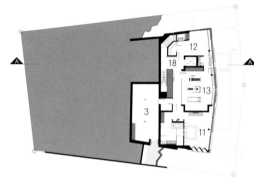

Fourth floor plan

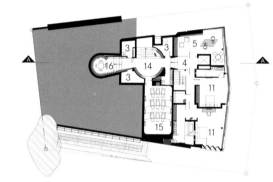

Fifth floor plan

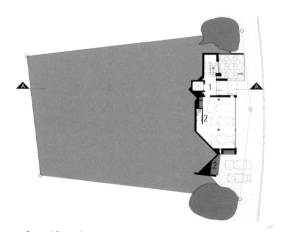

Ground floor plan

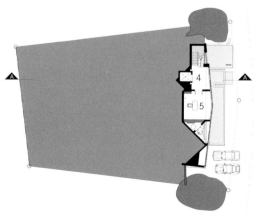

First floor plan

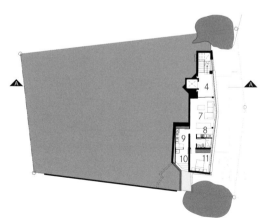

Second floor plan

Clad in walnut, the circular entrance area feels larger thanks to the fascinating light produced by the hanging glass backlights.

L'entrée, circulaire et recouverte en bois de noyer, s'agrandit grâce à l'illumination fascinante de la lumière de fond produite par du verre suspendu rétro-éclairé.

Der Eingangsbereich, rund und mit Nussbaumholz verkleidet, vergrößert sich dank der faszinierenden Beleuchtung mit Hintergrundlicht, das durch leuchtendes hängendes Glas entsteht.

La espacio de entrada, circular y revestido en madera de nogal, se amplifica gracias a la fascinante iluminación con luz de fondo producida mediante vidrios colgantes retroiluminados.

M 11 HOUSE

a21studio
Ho Chi Minh City, Vietnam
© Hiroyuki Oki

Through the use of natural materials—wood and stone—and overhead lighting, and the placement of small green courtyards inside the house, a21studio has designed elegant and peaceful spaces in which the owner can leave the stresses of the working day behind and enjoy his own space within the noisy and polluted atmosphere of Ho Chi Minh City.

Grâce à l'emploi de matériaux naturels – tels que le bois et la pierre –, l'utilisation de lumières en hauteur et de petites cours verdoyantes dans la maison, a21studio conçoit des espaces élégants et calmes pour que le propriétaire puisse oublier sa longue journée de travail éreintante, et profiter d'un espace personnel dans un environnement aussi bruyant et contaminé que peut l'être la ville de Ho Chi Minh.

Durch die Verwendung natürlicher Materialien – Holz und Stein –, die Nutzung des Lichtes von oben und die Einrichtung kleiner grüner Patios innerhalb des Hauses entwirft a21studio elegante und friedvolle Räume, damit der Eigentümer einen langen anstrengenden Arbeitstag hinter sich lassen und in einem so lauten und schmutzigen Umfeld wie Ho Chi Minh Stadt seinen eigenen Raum genießen kann.

Mediante el uso de materiales naturales –madera y piedra–, la utilización de luces superiores y la colocación de pequeños patios verdes dentro de la casa, a21studio diseña espacios elegantes y pacíficos para que el propietario pueda dejar atrás un largo día de trabajo agotador, y disfrutar de un espacio propio dentro un ambiente tan ruidoso y contaminado como es el de la ciudad de Ho Chi Minh.

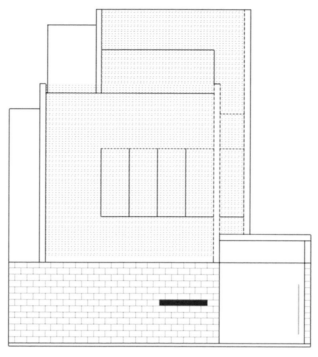

Elevation

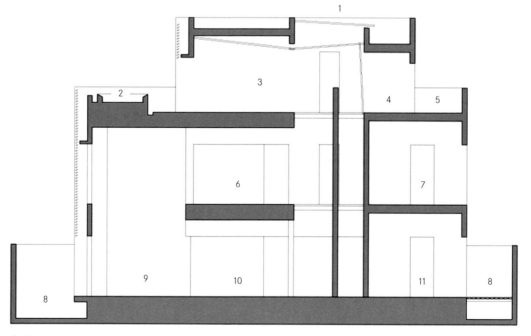

Section

1. Glass room
2. Pond
3. Gym
4. Bathroom
5. Rock garden
6. Family room
7. Master bedroom
8. Garden
9. Living room
10. Dining room
11. Bedroom

Used extensively throughout the house, the wood aims to soften the effect of the concrete floor and the huge column that dominates the centre of the house.

Le bois, largement utilisé dans toute la maison, a pour but d'adoucir le rôle du sol en béton et celui de la colonne colossale qui domine le centre de la maison.

Das im gesamten Wohnhaus großzügig eingesetzte Holz dient dem Ziel, die Dominanz des Betonbodens und der kolossalen Säule in der Mitte des Hauses zu entschärfen und aufzuweichen.

La madera, utilizada ampliamente en toda la vivienda, tiene el objetivo de suavizar el protagonismo del suelo de hormigón y el de la colosal columna que domina en el núcleo de la casa.

The small area taken up by this tree allows the sound of its leaves to be captured and resonate between the walls, bringing back the memories of the owner's birth city.

Le petit espace qu'occupe l'arbre permet que le son de ses feuilles soit emprisonné entre les murs, qu'il résonne et rappelle au propriétaire les souvenirs de sa ville natale.

Der reduzierte Raum, in dem der Baum wächst, ermöglicht es, dass der Klang seiner Blätter durch die Wände eingefangen wird, nachhallt und Erinnerungen an die Geburtsstadt des Eigentümers wach werden lässt.

El reducido espacio que ocupa el árbol permite que el sonido de sus hojas sea capturado entre las paredes, resuene y traiga de vuelta los recuerdos de la ciudad natal del propietario.

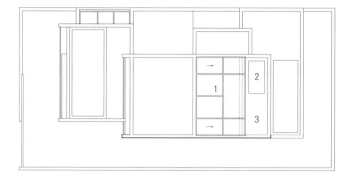

Roof plan

Second floor plan

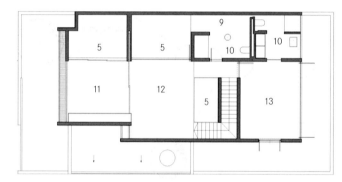

First floor plan

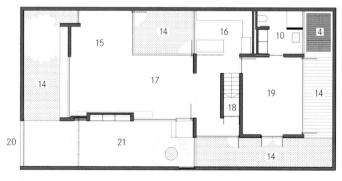

Ground floor plan

1. Glass roof
2. Water tank
3. Solar water heater
4. Pond
5. Void
6. Laundry
7. Gym
8. Bathroom
9. Rock garden
10. Toilet
11. Child room
12. Family room
13. Master bedroom
14. Garden
15. Living room
16. Kitchen
17. Dining room
18. Storage room
19. Bedroom
20. Entrance
21. Parking

THE LIGHTHOUSE 65

AR Design Studio
Hill Head, Fareham, United Kingdom
© Martin Gardner
www.spacialimages.com

Located on the south coast of England, this luxurious three-bedroom home enjoys a privileged position providing wonderful views of the Solent and the Isle of Wight, in the English Channel. Facing the beach, this interesting design by AR Design Studio takes inspiration from traditional beach pavilions such as De La Warr in nearby Bexhill.

Située sur la côte sud de l'Angleterre, cette luxueuse maison de trois pièces bénéficie d'une situation privilégiée qui lui permet d'avoir une vue merveilleuse sur Solent et l'île de Wight, dans le Canal de la Manche. Face à la plage, la conception intéressante d'AR Design Studio s'inspire des pavillons de plage traditionnels comme celui De La Warr à proximité de Bexhill.

An der Südküste Englands gelegen genießt dieses luxuriöse Wohnhaus mit drei Zimmern eine privilegierte Lage, sodass es einen wunderschönen Blick auf Solent und die Insel Wight im Ärmelkanal hat. Dem Strand zugewandt lässt sich der interessante Entwurf von AR Design Studio durch die traditionellen Strandpavillons, wie dem De La Warr im nahe gelegenen Bexhill, inspirieren.

Ubicada en la costa sur de Inglaterra, esta lujosa vivienda de tres habitaciones disfruta de una situación privilegiada que le permite contar con unas vistas maravillosas de Solent y de la isla de Wight, en el Canal de la Mancha. Orientada hacia la playa, el interesante diseño de AR Design Studio coge la inspiración de los tradicionales pabellones de playa como el De La Warr en la cercana Bexhill.

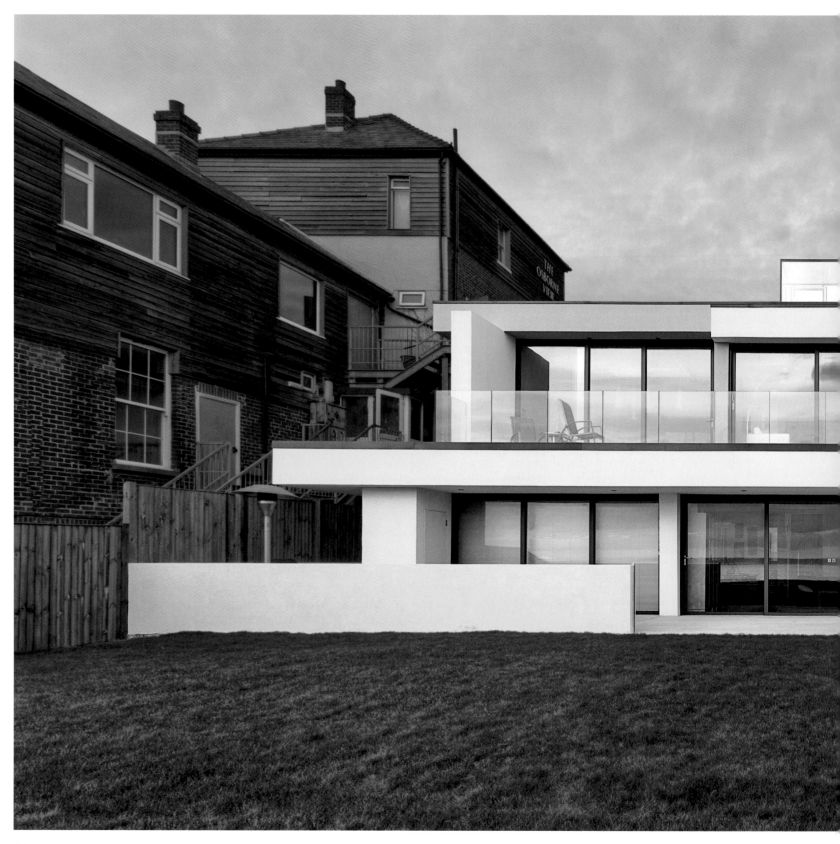

The house is seven metres below the road level, which allows the roof to act as a parking area for three cars.

La maison se trouve à sept mètres en dessous du niveau de la route, ce qui permet au toit de faire office de parking pour trois voitures maximum.

Das Haus befindet sich sieben Meter unter dem Niveau des Weges, wodurch das Dach als Parkplatz für bis zu drei Autos dienen kann.

La casa se encuentra siete metros por debajo del nivel del camino, lo cual permite que el techo actúe como un estacionamiento para hasta tres coches.

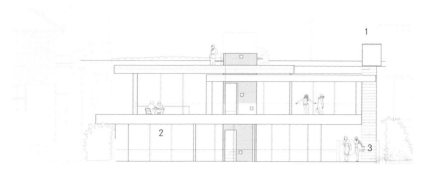

South elevation

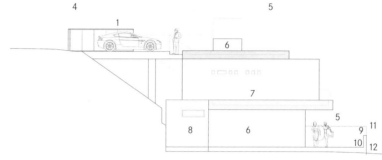

East elevation

1. Bin/Bike storage
2. Flood defence wall
   + 5.00 AOD
3. Stairs
4. Garage No. 63
5. No. 63 Marine cottage
6. White render
7. Grey render
8. DK grey render
9. Waterproof structural
   glass wall
10. Flood defence wall
11. + 5.00 AOD
12. + 3.25 AOD
13. Osborne view pub
14. Grey render to roof
15. White render to roof
16. Etched glass window
17. Copper cladding
18. Stair outline
19. + 3.60 AOD

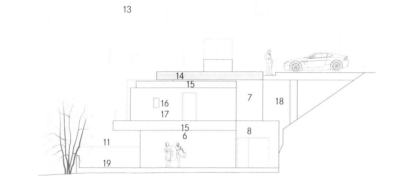

West elevation

Section AA'

1. Utility room
2. Living room
3. Balcony
4. Garden lounge

The glass cube is the main access and automatically reflects the local weather conditions according to the colour of its lighting: green for stable conditions and red for low pressure.

Le cube en verre est l'accès principal et indique automatiquement les conditions météorologiques locales en fonction de la couleur de son éclairage : vert pour un climat stable, rouge pour les basses pressions.

Der Glaswürfel ist der Hauptzugang und er zeigt durch die Farbe seiner Beleuchtung automatisch die lokalen meteorologischen Bedingungen an: Grün für stabile Wetterlage, Rot für Tiefdruck.

El cubo de vidrio es el acceso principal e indica automáticamente las condiciones meteorológicas locales en función del color de su iluminación: verde para clima estable, rojo para bajas presiones.

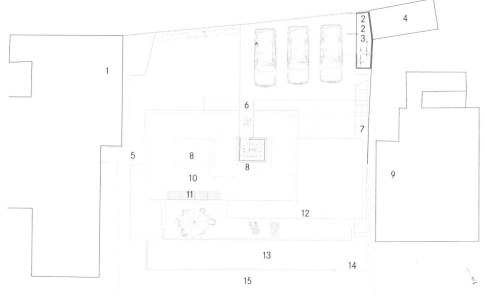

Site plan

1. Osborne view
2. Bin
3. Bike storage
4. Garage No. 63
5. Osborne view fire escape
6. Bridge
7. Stairs
8. Roof light
9. No. 63 Marine cottage
10. Grass roof
11. Louvers
12. Pebbles to roof
13. + 3.60 AOD
14. Removable flood gate
15. Flood gate to
    + 5.00 AOD

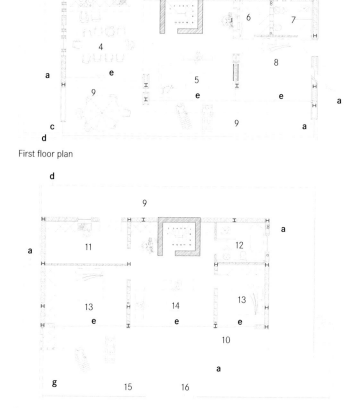

First floor plan

Ground floor plan

1. Kitchen
2. Utility room
3. Toilet
4. Dining room
5. Living room
6. Dressing room
7. Ensuite
8. Master bedroom
9. Balcony
10. Patio
11. Store/Utility room
12. Bathroom
13. Bedroom
14. Garden lounge
15. Flood defence wall
16. Flood defence gate

a. Roof over
b. SVP
c. Structural glass
   balustrade
d. Parapet wall
e. Sliding doors
f. Building over
g. Retaining wall

162

The design maximises the width of the building and ensures that each room and living space enjoys extensive views over the coastline.

La conception permet d'optimiser la largeur du bâtiment et que chaque pièce et chaque partie commune puisse profiter de larges vues sur la côte.

Es gelingt dem Entwurf, die Breite des Gebäudes zu maximieren sodass jedes Zimmer und jeder Wohnraum einen weiten Blick auf die Küste bietet.

El diseño consigue maximizar el ancho del edificio y que cada habitación y espacio de vida pueda disfrutar de amplias vistas sobre la costa.

PERIBERE RESIDENCE

[STRANG] Architecture
Miami, Florida, United States
© Bruce Buck, © Claudia Uribe-Touri

Despite the fascinating privacy of the entrance, the interior of this [STRANG] Architecture project it is a perfect combination of space, light and transparency. The culmination of the connection between inside and out, and the sweeping views over the Bay of Biscayne and the Miami skyline, are a veritable feast for the eye.

Malgré l'intimité fascinante de l'entrée, l'intérieur de la maison conçue par [STRANG] Architecture est une combinaison parfaite entre l'espace, la lumière et les transparences. Sans aucun doute, le point culminant du lien entre l'intérieur et l'extérieur de la maison, et où les impressionnantes vue sur la baie de Biscayne et le skyline de Miami attirent le regard.

Trotz der faszinierenden Privatsphäre des Einganges, ist das Interieur des durch [STRANG] Architecture entworfenen Hauses eine perfekte Konjugation des Raumes, des Lichts und der Transparenz. Zweifelsohne ist der Gipfel der Verbindung zwischen Innen- und Außenbereich des Hauses, da wo sich weite Blicke über die Bucht von Biscayne und auf die Skyline von Miami bieten, ein Blickfang.

Pese a la fascinante privacidad de la entrada, el interior de la vivienda diseñada por [STRANG] Architecture es una conjugación perfecta de espacio, de luz y de transparencias. Sin duda, la culminación de la conexión entre el interior y el exterior de la vivienda, y donde las amplias vistas sobre la bahía de Biscayne y el perfil de los edificios de Miami son un imán para la vista.

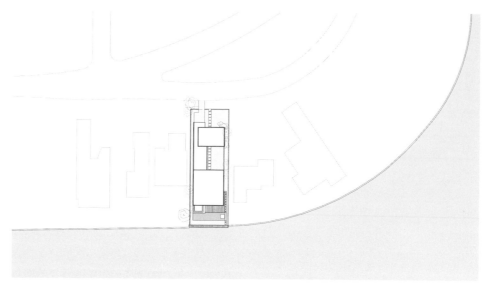

Site plan

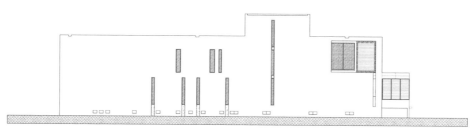

Section

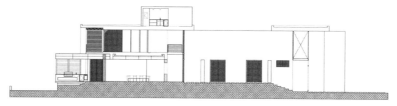

Elevation

The raised interior courtyard gives the house the sense and comfort that one would associate with a garden lifestyle.

La terrasse intérieure surélevée donne à la maison l'aspect et le confort d'un mode de vie en osmose avec le jardin.

Der erhöhte Innenhof verleiht dem Haus das Aussehen und die Annehmlichkeit eines mit dem Garten verbundenen Lebensstils.

El patio interior elevado proporciona a la vivienda el aspecto y la comodidad de un estilo de vida conectado con el jardín.

Rising above the ground, the house is able to fight the tide of occasional hurricanes and address the long-term challenges of the rising sea level.

La maison, surélevée par rapport au terrain, arrive à lutter contre la houle des ouragans occasionnels et à mieux affronter à long terme les défis de la montée des eaux.

Dadurch, dass sich das Haus über das Grundstück erhebt, können ihm die Sturzseen der gelegentlichen Hurrikans nichts anhaben und auf lange Sicht kann es den Herausforderungen eines steigenden Meeresspiegels besser trotzen.

La vivienda, al levantarse sobre el terreno, logra combatir la marejada de los huracanes ocasionales y afrontar mejor los desafíos a largo plazo de la subida del nivel del mar.

First floor plan

Ground floor plan

HOUSE C

zaettastudio architettura e design
Treviso, Italy
© Alberto Ferrero

The villa is built in a strategic location in which it is able to face the world like a two-sided sculpture: on one side the street access, facing the town; on the other the private garden, facing the valley and hills of Montello. This project by Giorgio Zaetta hides itself from urban view, while opening itself up with a large panoramic window on the opposite side.

La villa est construite sur un lieu stratégique qui lui permet de contempler le monde comme une sculpture à deux visages : d'un côté, l'accès à la rue, en direction du village; de l'autre, le jardin privé, en direction de la vallée et des collines de Montello. Le projet de Giorgio Zaetta cache sa position du côté de la rue, tandis que du côté opposé, elle s'ouvre grâce à une grande fenêtre panoramique.

Die Villa wurde an einem strategischen Ort erbaut, der es ermöglicht, die Welt als Skulptur mit zwei Gesichtern zu betrachten: Auf der einen Seite der Zugang zur Straße, zum Dorf ausgerichtet; auf der anderen der private Garten, der zum Tal und den Hügeln von Montello hin liegt. Das Projekt von Giorgio Zaetta verbirgt seine Lage auf der dem Ort zugewandten Seite, während es sich zur entgegengesetzten Seite mit einem großen Panoramafenster öffnet.

La villa está construida en un lugar estratégico que le permite contemplar el mundo como una escultura de dos caras: por un lado, el acceso a la calle, orientado hacia el pueblo; por otro, el jardín privado, orientado hacia el valle y las colinas de Montello. El proyecto de Giorgio Zaetta oculta su posición por el lado urbano, mientras que se abre con una gran ventana panorámica en el lado opuesto.

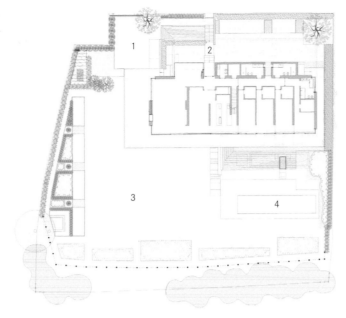

Site plan

1. Driveway access
2. Pedestrian access
3. Private garden
4. Swimming pool

Higher floor plan

Ground floor plan

With the help of strategically placed lighting at its base, the house appears to be almost magically suspended over the ground.

La maison, grâce à un éclairage stratégiquement situé à sa base, apparait de façon presque magique suspendue sur le terrain.

Das Haus scheint mithilfe der strategisch unten angelegten Beleuchtung auf beinah magische Weise über dem Boden zu schweben.

La vivienda, con la ayuda de una iluminación situada estratégicamente en su base, aparece en una suspensión sobre el terreno casi mágica.

Facing directly onto the widest part of the terrace, the living room occupies the entire southern side of the upper floor with views on three sides.

Le salon, directement situé face à la partie la plus large de la terrasse, occupe toute la zone sud de l'étage supérieur et à des vues sur trois directions.

Der Salon, der dem breitesten Teil der Terrasse direkt gegenüberliegt, beansprucht den gesamten südlichen Bereich des oberen Stockwerks und bietet Ausblicke in drei verschiedene Richtungen.

El salón, enfrentado directamente a la parte más ancha de la terraza, ocupa toda la zona sur de la planta superior y cuenta con vistas en tres direcciones.

IN PRAISE OF SHADOWS

Pitsou Kedem Architects
Tel Aviv-Yafo, Israel
© Amit Geron

The use of steel on the façade is undoubtedly the most striking feature of this design by Pitsou Kedem Architects. Mass and space are combined in the big steel structure which, like a sculpture, is integrated into the façade, creating and establishing clear boundaries for the home. Light and shadows enhance the feeling of space and add a certain air of mystery.

L'utilisation de l'acier dans la façade est, sans doute, la caractéristique la plus frappante de la conception de Pitsou Kedem Architects. La masse et l'espace se marient dans la grande structure en acier qui, telle une sculpture, s'intègre dans la façade en permettant de créer et d'établir des limites claires pour la maison. La lumière et les ombres amplifient l'espace et donnent un certain mystère.

Die Verwendung von Stahl in der Fassade ist zweifelsohne das auffälligste Merkmal des Designs von Pitsou Kedem Architects. Masse und Raum werden in der großen Stahlstruktur kombiniert, die sich wie eine Skulptur in die Fassade integriert und eine klare Abgrenzung des Hauses nach außen entstehen lässt und bildet. Licht und Schatten steigern so noch das Raumerlebnis und verleihen dem Ganzen etwas Geheimnisvolles.

La utilización del acero en la fachada es, sin duda, la característica más llamativa del diseño de Pitsou Kedem Architects. Masa y espacio se combinan en la gran estructura de acero que, como una escultura, se integra en la fachada y permite que se creen y establezcan límites claros para el hogar. Luces y sombras mejoran así la experiencia del espacio y proporcionan un cierto misterio.

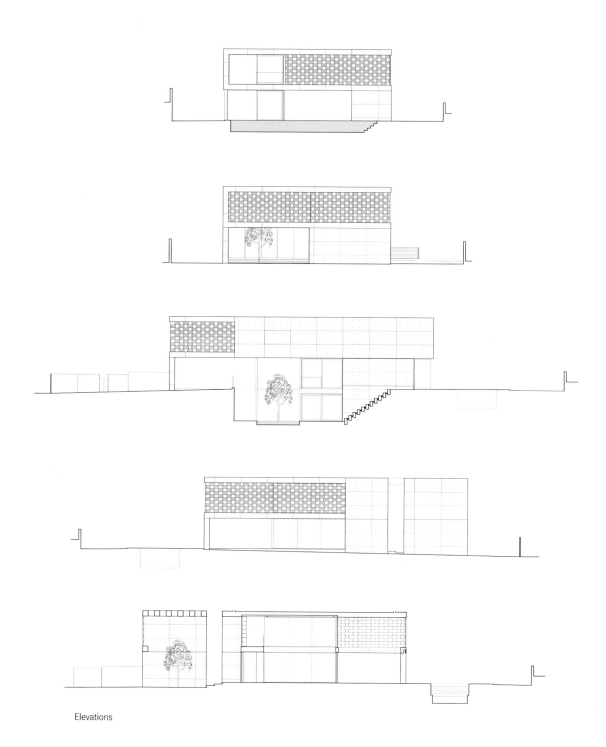

Elevations

The building is constructed with large, inanimate exposed concrete walls which, without the movement of light and shadows, would seem almost monastic.

Le bâtiment est construit avec des murs en béton visibles, grands et inanimés qui, sans le mouvement de la lumière et des ombres, paraîtraient presque monastique.

Das Gebäude wurde aus Sichtbetonmauern errichtet, groß und leblos, die ohne die Bewegungen von Licht und Schatten beinah klösterlich wirken.

El edificio está construido con muros de hormigón visto, grandes e inanimados que, sin el movimiento de las luces y las sombras, parecería casi monástico.

PEARL BAY RESIDENCE

Gavin Maddock Design Studio
Yzerfontein, South Africa
© Adam Letch

With a bank of sand dunes sitting higher than the rest of the land plot, Gavin Maddock Design Studio's challenge was to consolidate the house, the dunes and the ocean views. In this privileged natural setting, the rectangular two-floored holiday house imaginatively conceives its outdoor living spaces and will, ultimately, serve as the owner's retreat.

Avec un front de dunes un peu plus élevé que le reste du terrain, le défi de Gavin Maddock Design Studio a été de concilier la maison, les dunes et les vues sur l'océan. Sur un site naturel privilégié, cette maison de vacances, entièrement rectangulaire et à deux étages, conçoit de manière imaginative les parties communes extérieures qui, serviront finalement, de lieu de retraite au propriétaire.

Angesichts der Dünen, die etwas höher als der Rest des Grundstücks sind, sah sich Gavin Maddock Design Studio vor der Herausforderung, Wohnhaus, Dünen und Meerblick in Einklang zu bringen. Dieses in einer privilegierten natürlichen Umgebung gelegene Ferienhaus, vollkommen rechtwinklig und zweistöckig, konzipiert die Lebensräume außen auf fantasievolle Weise, die später dem Eigentümer als Rückzugsort dienen sollen.

Con un frente de dunas algo más alto que el resto del terreno, el reto de Gavin Maddock Design Studio fue conciliar vivienda, dunas y vistas sobre el océano. En un paraje natural privilegiado, esta casa de vacaciones, totalmente rectangular y de dos plantas, concibe de forma imaginativa los espacios de vida exteriores que, a la larga, servirán como lugar de retiro al propietario.

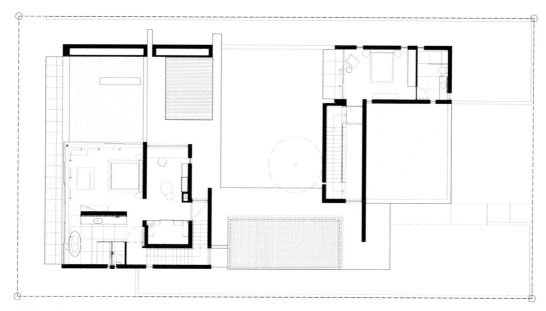

First floor plan

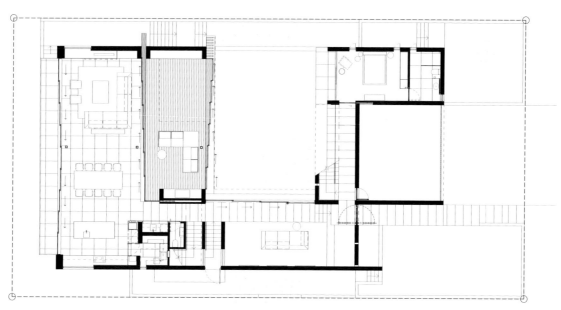

Ground floor plan

Proportion and height are essential in this design. The high ceilings and full-height sliding doors provide lightness and space inside, and a connection with the exterior.

La proportion et la hauteur sont essentielles dans la conception. Les hauts plafonds et les portes coulissantes pleine hauteur permettent de donner de la légèreté à l'espace intérieur et de faire le lien avec l'extérieur.

Proportion und Höhe spielen beim Design eine ausschlaggebende Rolle. Die hohen Decken und die Schiebetüren über die gesamte Höhe verleihen dem Innenraum Leichtigkeit und verbinden ihn mit dem Außen.

Proporción y altura son esenciales en el diseño. Los altos techos y las puertas correderas de altura completa permiten proporcionar ligereza al espacio interior y conectarlo con el exterior.

PLANE HOUSE

k-studio
Skiathos Island, Sporades Islands, Greece
© Yiorgos Kordakis

Summer in the Greek islands is for living it up and enjoying the fresh air. This design by k-studio avoids large shapes that divide and dominate the space. In their place are flat, horizontal shapes that are set into the slope providing differentiated areas on different levels for sunbathing, sleeping and eating, as well as open spaces with plenty of shade.

Sans aucun doute, l'été est fait dans les îles grecques, pour s'amuser et pour profiter d'activités en plein air. La conception de k-studio évite les grands volumes qui divisent et dominent l'espace. Au lieu de cela, des plans horizontaux construits dans la pente donnent, à différents niveaux, des espaces contrastés pour prendre le soleil, dormir et manger; ainsi que des espaces ouverts où l'ombre prédomine.

Im Sommer auf den griechischen Inseln spielt sich das Leben zweifelsohne an der frischen Luft ab. Der Entwurf von k-studio vermeidet große Blöcke, die den Raum zerteilen und dominieren. Stattdessen bieten in den Hang eingebaute horizontale Flächen auf unterschiedlichen Ebenen verschiedene Bereiche zum Sonnen, Schlafen und Essen, sowie offene Bereiche, in denen der Schatten dominiert.

El verano en las isla griegas es, sin duda, para vivirlo y disfrutarlo al aire libre. El diseño de k-studio evita los grandes volúmenes que dividen y dominan el espacio. En su lugar, planos horizontales insertados en la pendiente proporcionan, en distintos niveles, zonas diferenciadas para tomar el sol, dormir y comer; así como zonas abiertas donde predomina la sombra.

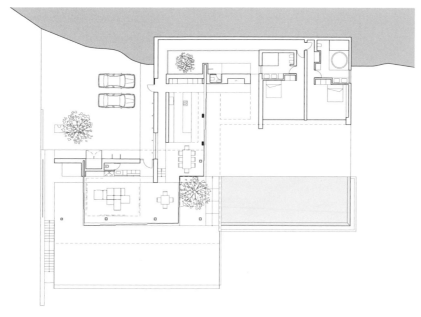

Upper level floor plan

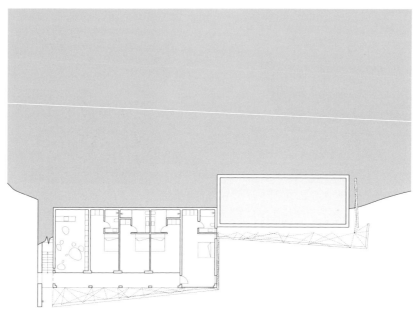

Lower level floor plan

The intelligent furniture solutions, with mobile units mounted on rails, creates dynamism by blurring the boundaries between inside and out.

La solution intelligente des meubles, avec des unités mobiles montées sur rails, permet un grand dynamisme car les limites entre l'espace intérieur et extérieur sont estompées.

Die intelligente Lösung des Mobiliars, mit beweglichen auf Schienen befestigten Einheiten, erlaubt große Dynamik und lässt zugleich die Grenzen zwischen Innen- und Außenräumen verwischen.

La inteligente solución del mobiliario, con unidades móviles montadas en raíles, permite un gran dinamismo al quedar difuminados los límites entre el espacio interior y el exterior.

BEAUMARIS WHITE HOUSE

In2
Melbourne, Victoria, Australia
© Dean Schmideg

In2 has adopted a minimalist design philosophy in this project. The shapes of the different spaces are adapted to suit their function, without resorting to extra embellishments to improve the architecture. The house delivers a cohesive and timeless solution in which every aspect, from the finishes to the arrangement of the rooms, has been considered accurately and meticulously.

Dans ce projet, In2 adopte une philosophie de conception minimaliste. Les formes du bâtiment s'adaptent à la fonction des espaces, sans avoir recours à des ornements supplémentaires pour améliorer son architecture. La maison répond à une solution très cohérente et intemporelle où tous les aspects, des finitions aux dispositions des pièces, ont été analysées de manière précise et méticuleuse.

Bei diesem Projekt wendet In2 eine Philosophie minimalistischen Designs an. Die Formen des Gebäudes passen sich an die Funktion der Räume an, ohne auf die Architektur verbessernde verschönernde Extras zurückzugreifen. Das Haus ist eine sehr kompakte und zeitlose Lösung, bei der alle Aspekte, vom Finish bis zur Lage der Zimmer, aufs Genaueste geplant und bedacht wurden.

En este proyecto, In2 adopta una filosofía de diseño minimalista. Las formas del edificio se adaptan a la función de los espacios, sin recurrir a embellecimientos extras que mejoren su arquitectura. La vivienda responde a una solución muy cohesionada y atemporal donde todos los aspectos, desde los acabados hasta la disposición de las habitaciones, han sido considerados de forma precisa y meticulosa.

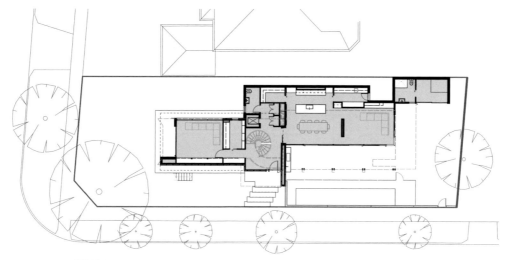

Site plan

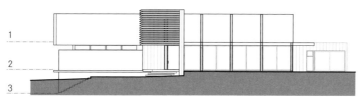

West elevation

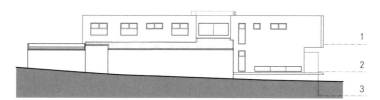

East elevation

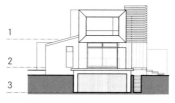

North elevation

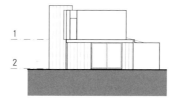

South elevation

1. First floor
2. Ground floor
3. Basement

Supported on a lighter structure, the house's large, monolithic, solid cubic forms give the impression of being suspended.

Les grandes formes cubiques monolithiques et solides qui composent la maison semblent être suspendues dans l'air car elles reposent sur une structure plus légère.

Die großen monolithischen und soliden kubischen Formen, aus denen das Haus besteht, wirken dadurch, dass sie durch eine leichtere Konstruktion getragen werden, als würden sie schweben.

Las grandes formas cúbicas monolíticas y sólidas que componen la vivienda, al estar apoyadas sobre una estructura más ligera, parece que se encuentren en suspensión.

A holistic approach ensures that all the interior spaces fulfil their original function and reflect the bold and minimalist design aesthetic of the building.

Une approche holistique assure que tous les espaces intérieurs remplissent leur fonction d'origine et reflètent esthétiquement la conception audacieuse et minimaliste du bâtiment.

Ein ganzheitlicher Ansatz stellt sicher, dass alle Innenräume ihre ursprüngliche Funktion erfüllen und die Ästhetik des kühnen und minimalistischen Designs des Gebäudes widerspiegeln.

Un enfoque holístico asegura que todos los espacios interiores cumplan con su función original y reflejen la estética de diseño audaz y minimalista del edificio.

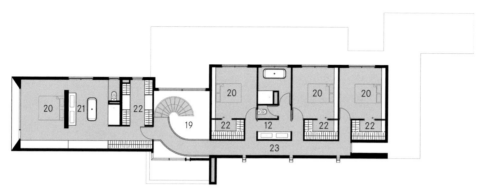

First floor plan

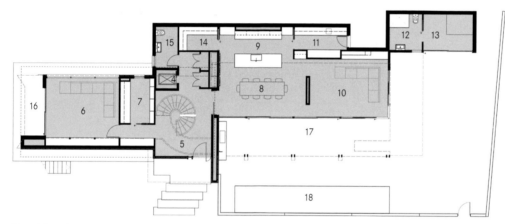

Ground floor plan

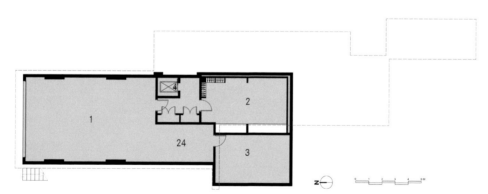

Basement floor plan

1. Parking	13. Gym/Sauna
2. Bar/Cellar	14. Pantry
3. Store room	15. Powder room
4. Lift	16. Balcony
5. Entrance	17. Patio
6. Living room	18. Swimming pool
7. Study	19. Void
8. Dining room	20. Bedroom
9. Kitchen	21. Ensuite
10. Family room	22. Dressing room
11. Laundry	23. Passage
12. Bathroom	24. Workshop

VILLA K

at26
Bratislava, Slovak Republic
© at26

Despite the constraints of the small plot size, the spatial and functional composition of this house fully embodies the client's wishes. The result is a complex design: the first two floors follow an L-shaped arrangement; the third follows the edge of the plot; and the fourth is inset as a superstructure with a terrace.

La structure spatiale et fonctionnelle de la maison, en dépit d'être limitée par la taille réduite du terrain, matérialise totalement les désirs des clients. Il en résulte une conception complexe : dans les deux premiers étages, l'agencement de la maison est en forme de L ; le troisième étage suit la forme du terrain et le quatrième est encastré comme une superstructure avec terrasse.

Die räumliche und funktionale Komposition dieses Hauses, wenngleich durch die begrenzte Grundstücksfläche bedingt, erfüllt die Wünsche des Auftraggebers vollständig. Das Ergebnis ist ein komplexer Entwurf: Die beiden ersten Stockwerke haben eine L-Form; das dritte folgt dem Rand des Grundstücks und das vierte befindet sich darauf als Überbau mit Terrasse.

La composición espacial y funcional de la vivienda, pese a estar condicionada por el tamaño reducido del terreno, materializa completamente los deseos del cliente. El resultado es un diseño complejo: en las dos primeras plantas, el cuerpo se define en una disposición en forma de L; la tercera sigue el borde del terreno y la cuarta se encuentra empotrada como una superestructura con terraza.

The ground is slightly uneven, allowing the living room to be partially located below ground.

Le terrain est en léger dénivellement, ce qui fait que le salon se trouve en partie en dessous du niveau du sol.

Das Grundstück ist leicht uneben, wodurch der Wohnraum teilweise unter Bodenniveau liegen kann.

El terreno del lugar está ligeramente desnivelado, lo que permite que la sala de estar se encuentre parcialmente por debajo del suelo.

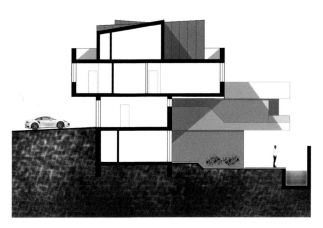

Section

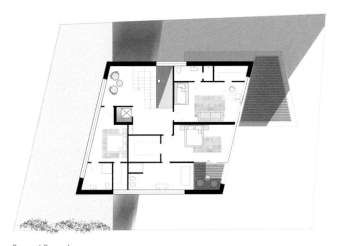

Second floor plan

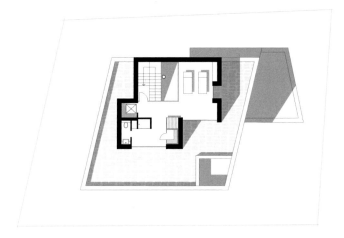

Roof plan

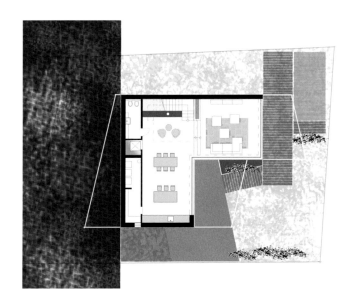

Ground floor plan

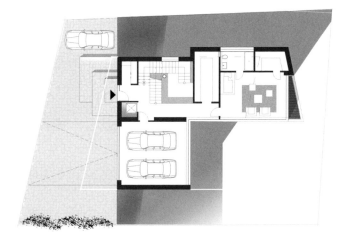

First floor plan

With the superstructure on the terrace, the house maintains its vertical alignment with the surrounding buildings.

Avec l'ajout de la superstructure sur la terrasse, la maison parvient à conserver l'alignement vertical avec les bâtiments alentours.

Mit dem Aufbau auf der Terrasse gelingt es, die vertikale Fluchtlinie mit den benachbarten Gebäuden beizubehalten.

Con la incorporación de la superestructura en la terraza, la vivienda consigue mantener la alineación vertical con los edificios de alrededor.

LAKE UNION FLOAT HOUSE

Dan Nelson AIA, Designs Northwest Architects, Shawn Sullivan
Lake Union, Seattle, Washington, United States
© Ben Benschneider

The client's original intention was to 'fit in' with the neighbours by mimicking the prevailing artisan style. After walking around the docks, however, he decided to embrace a more natural reference by emulating the marina's distinctive warehouses: large box-like structures whose appearance has barely changed for years and which dominate the coastline from Seattle.

Au départ, l'intention du client était de "cadrer" avec les voisins en imitant le style artisanal dominant. Après s'être promené sur les quais, il a décidé, cependant, d'adopter une référence plus naturelle : imiter les magasins typiques des quais du port de plaisance. De grandes structures en forme de cube, qui n'ont guère changé d'apparence au fil du temps, et qui sont dominantes sur la ligne côtière de Seattle.

Die erste Intention des Eigentümers war es, sich durch Imitation des herrschenden handwerklichen Stils in die Nachbarschaft „einzufügen". Nach dem Gang über die Mole entschied er sich jedoch, eine natürlichere Referenz zu übernehmen: Den typischen Speichern der Molen des Sporthafens nachzueifern. Große kastenförmige Strukturen, deren Aussehen sich im Lauf der Zeit kaum verändert hat, und die die Küstenlinie von Seattle an dominieren.

La intención inicial del cliente era "encajar" con los vecinos al imitar el estilo artesano imperante. Después de caminar por los muelles, sin embargo, decidió adoptar una referencia más natural: emular a los típicos almacenes de los muelles del puerto deportivo. Grandes estructuras en forma de caja, que han variado poco la apariencia con el tiempo, y que dominan la línea de costa desde Seattle.

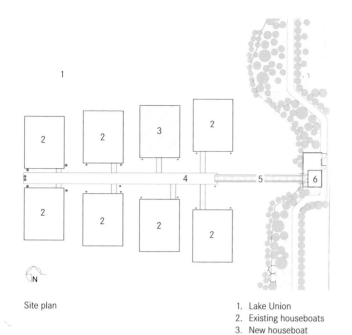

Site plan

1. Lake Union
2. Existing houseboats
3. New houseboat
4. Gangway
5. Ramp
6. Entrance pavilion

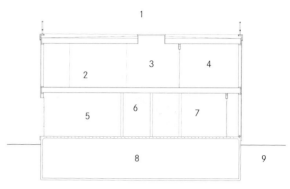

Section

1. Rooftop deck
2. Sitting room
3. Stair hall
4. Guest room
5. Living room
6. Study (Kitchen beyond)
7. Entry
8. Float
9. Water

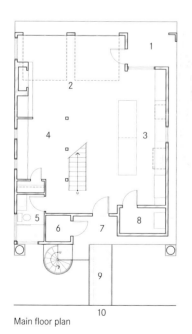

Main floor plan

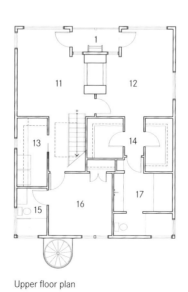

Upper floor plan

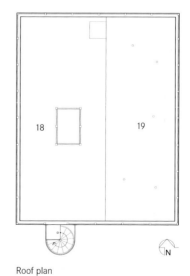

Roof plan

1. Deck
2. Living room
3. Kitchen
4. Office
5. Bathroom
6. Storage room
7. Entrance
8. Mechanical room
9. Gangway
10. Mainland
11. Sitting room
12. Master bedroom
13. Laundry
14. Master closet
15. Guest bathroom
16. Guest bedroom
17. Master bathroom
18. Rooftop deck
19. Putting green

The ground floor is an open space, which establishes a strong and close connection with the ocean outside thanks to its heavy-duty glass doors.

Le rez-de-chaussée est un espace lumineux qui, grâce à de grandes portes en verre qui basculent, parvient à créer une connexion intense et forte avec le milieu marin extérieur.

Die untere Etage ist ein durchsichtiger Raum, der mittels großer Schwingtore aus Glas eine starke und enge Verbindung zum marinen Umfeld schafft.

La planta baja es un espacio diáfano que, mediante unas grandes puertas basculantes de vidrio, consigue establecer una fuerte y estrecha conexión con el exterior marino.

PRODROMOS AND DESI RESIDENCE

VARDASTUDIO architects + designers
Tala, Cyprus
© Creative Photo Room

In Vardastudio's design the different areas of the house are configured vertically; entrance, privacy and views all take advantage of the plot's natural characteristics. Based on this, the individual structures of each floor, the parking area, the terraces and the pool are all arranged downwards, while from the street the house has the discreet appearance of being a single floor.

La conception de Vardastudio structure à la verticale les différents espaces de la maison; elle utilise la morphologie du terrain pour y accéder, pour protéger son intimité et avoir des vues. Suivant ces critères, les volumes individuels de chaque étage, le parking, les terrasses et la piscine se dessinent vers le bas, alors que de la rue la résidence montre la présence discrète d'un seul étage.

Der Entwurf von Vardastudio konfiguriert die unterschiedlichen Räume des Wohnhauses in der Vertikalen; er nutzt die Morphologie des Grundstücks für den Zugang, die Privatsphäre und den Blick aus. Unter diesen Kriterien reihen sich die einzelnen Geschosse aneinander, vom Parkplatz über die Terrassen und den Pool nach unten, während es von der Straße aus wirkt wie ein bescheidenes einstöckiges Haus.

El diseño de Vardastudio configura en vertical los diferentes espacios de la vivienda; aprovecha la morfología del terreno para el acceso, la privacidad y las vistas. Con estos criterios, los volúmenes individuales de cada planta, el aparcamiento, las terrazas y la piscina se perfilan hacia abajo, mientras que desde la calle la residencia tiene la presencia discreta de una sola planta.

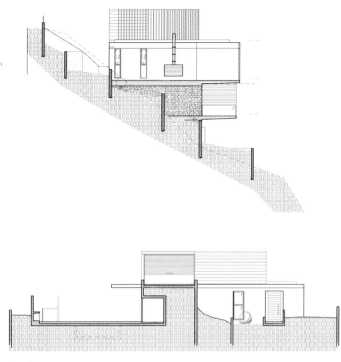

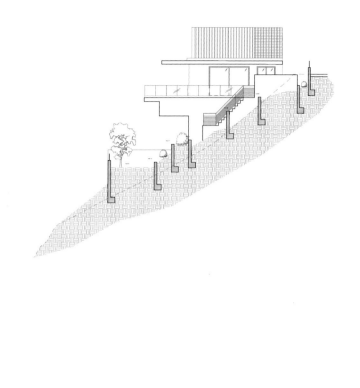

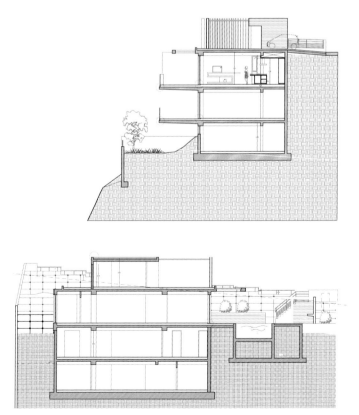

Elevations

Sections

The house's large concrete shapes seem to float on the side of the hill, creating an unexpected composition that seems to defy gravity.

Les grands volumes en béton de la maison semblent flotter sur le côté de la colline, en créant une structure inattendue qui semble défier la gravité.

Die großen Mengen an Beton scheinen neben dem Hügel zu schweben, so schaffen sie eine unerwartete Komposition, die der Schwerkraft nicht zu gehorchen scheint.

Los grandes volúmenes de hormigón de la vivienda parecen flotar en el lado de la colina, creando una composición inesperada que parece desafiar la gravedad.

The kitchen, living room and dining room have direct access to the pool and terrace, both of which are suspended via cantilevers and orientated towards the horizon.

La cuisine, le salon et la salle à manger ont un accès direct à la piscine et à la terrasse, toutes deux suspendues en porte-à-faux en direction de l'horizon.

Küche, Wohn- und Esszimmer haben direkten Zugang zu Pool und Terrasse, die beide als Vorsprünge Richtung Horizont angelegt sind.

La cocina, la sala de estar y el comedor tienen acceso directo a la piscina y la terraza, ambas situadas en un voladizo suspendido en dirección al horizonte.

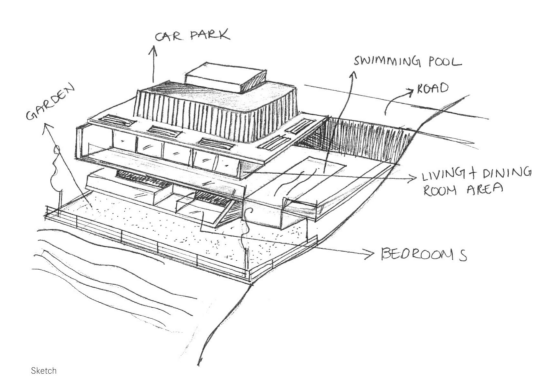

Sketch

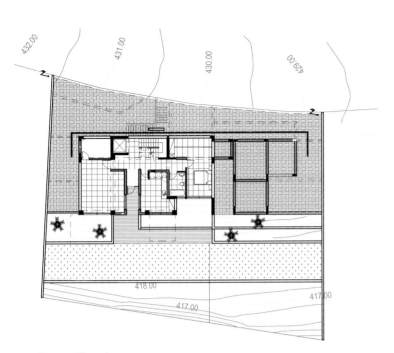

Basement floor plan

First lower level plan

Second lower level plan

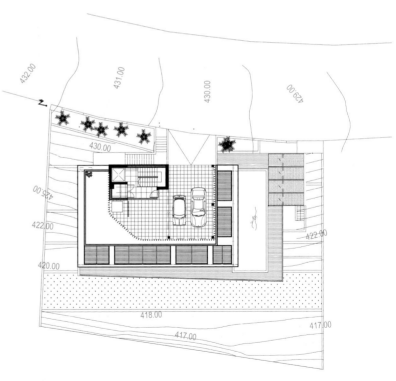

Garage – Road level

262

While the parking area is at street level, the house unravels in three lower levels, increasing in privacy towards the bottom.

Alors que le parking se trouve au niveau de la rue, la maison se situe sur trois niveaux inférieurs de plus en plus intimes au fur et à mesure que vous descendez.

Während sich der Parkplatz auf Straßenniveau befindet, erstreckt sich das Wohnhaus über drei darunterliegende Stockwerke, die immer intimer werden, je weiter man nach unten kommt.

Mientras que el aparcamiento se encuentra al nivel de la calle, la vivienda se desentraña en tres niveles inferiores, donde la intimidad es cada vez mayor a medida que se avanza hacia abajo.

BOLTON EAST

Naturhumaine
Bolton East, Quebec, Canada
© Adrien Williams + David Dworkind

Having bought a beautiful wooded plot in eastern Quebec, these clients dreamed of building a cottage that would be in perfect harmony with its natural environment. The steep slope culminates in a natural plateau just below the top, making it the perfect place for Naturhumaine to build the house.

Ayant acheté un beau terrain arboré dans l'est du Québec, les clients rêvaient de construire une maison de campagne qui serait en parfaite harmonie avec l'environnement naturel. Le terrain, en pente abrupte, culmine sur un plateau naturel juste en dessous du point le plus haut du lieu, ce qui en fait l'endroit idéal pour que Naturhumaine conçoive la maison.

Nach dem Erwerb eines schönen von Bäumen bestandenen Grundstücks im Osten von Quebec träumten die Eigentümer davon, ein Landhaus zu bauen, das sich in perfekter Symbiose mit der natürlichen Umgebung befindet. Das Gelände mit einem steilen Hang kulminiert in einer natürlichen Hochebene direkt unter dem höchsten Punkt des Terrains, wodurch dies zum perfekten Ort wird, wo Naturhumaine schließlich das Haus errichtet.

Habiendo comprado un bonito terreno poblado de árboles en el este del Quebec, los clientes soñaban con construir una casa de campo que se encontraría en perfecta simbiosis con el entorno natural. El terreno, con una pendiente escarpada, culmina en una meseta natural justo por debajo del punto más alto lugar, que lo convierten en la localización perfecta donde Naturhumaine levanta la vivienda.

The house comprises two stacked shapes. One is clad in wood and anchored into the mountain, while the other is cantilevered above it.

La maison est composée de deux volumes empilés. Un volume recouvert de bois ancré dans la montage, qui supporte un volume en porte-à-faux par dessus.

Das Haus besteht aus zwei übereinander gelagerten Körpern. Ein mit Holz verkleideter Körper ist im Berg verankert und trägt den anderen, über ihn herausragenden.

La vivienda está compuesta por dos volúmenes apilados. Un volumen revestido de madera anclado en la montaña, que soporta un volumen en voladizo por encima.

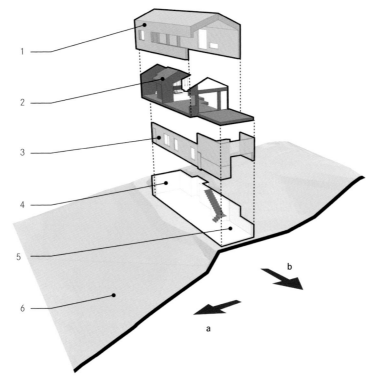

1. Gable roofed steel skin
2. Cantilevered living space
3. Base – wood skin
4. Embedded garden level
5. Parking
6. Sloped topography

a. View of the valley
b. View of Mount Orford

Exploded-axonometric view

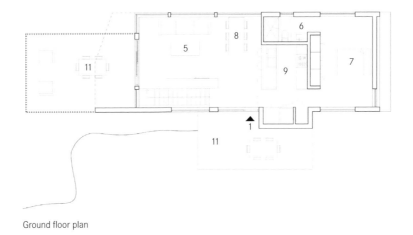

Ground floor plan

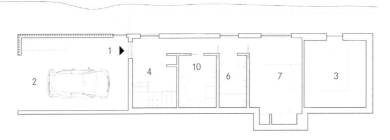

Garden level floor plan

1. Entrance	7. Bedroom
2. Parking	8. Dining room
3. Storage room	9. Kitchen
4. Vestibule	10. Mechanical
5. Living room	room
6. Bathroom	11. Terrace

The kitchen and bathroom are 'sculpted' in a black shape in the centre of the house, dividing the living spaces from the master bedroom.

La cuisine et la salle de bain sont "taillées" dans un volume noir au centre de la maison, et séparent les parties communes de la chambre principale.

Küche und Badezimmer sind in einen schwarzen Teil im Zentrum des Hauses „geschnitzt" und unterteilen die Wohnräume vom Hauptschlafzimmer aus.

La cocina y el baño están 'tallados' en un volumen negro en el centro de la vivienda, y dividen los espacios de vida desde el dormitorio principal.

SUMMER HOUSE ON PAROS

React Architects
Paros, Cyclades Islands, Greece
© Elias Chandelis

React Architects' aim was to create two holiday houses with views of the sea and the neighbouring island of Antiparos. The houses are located on the highest point of the land plot. The many courtyards and terraces act as a connective element between them, and the sweeping staircases that move between the interior and exterior spaces lead to 'plateaux' offering sweeping views of the landscape.

Le projet de React Architects est de concevoir deux maisons estivales qui donnent sur la mer et sur l'île voisine d'Antiparos. Les résidences sont situées sur le point le plus élevé du terrain ; les nombreuses cours et terrasses forment le trait d'union entre elles ; et les larges escaliers, qui traversent les espaces intérieurs et extérieurs, conduisent à des "plateaux" bénéficiant de vues panoramiques.

Der Entwurf von React Architects umfasst zwei Sommerhäuser mit Blick aufs Meer und die benachbarte Insel Antiparos. Die Häuser sind auf dem höchsten Punkt des Grundstücks gelegen; die vielen Patios und Terrassen bilden das verbindende Element zwischen ihnen; und die breiten Treppen, die Innen- und Außenräume durchqueren, führen zu „Plateaus" mit weitem Blick.

La propuesta de React Architects es el diseño de dos casas de verano, con vistas al mar y a la vecina isla de Antiparos. Las residencias se encuentran ubicadas en el punto más alto del terreno; los múltiples patios y terrazas constituyen el elemento conjuntivo entre ellas; y las amplias escaleras, que atraviesan espacios interiores y exteriores, conducen a "mesetas" con amplias vistas.

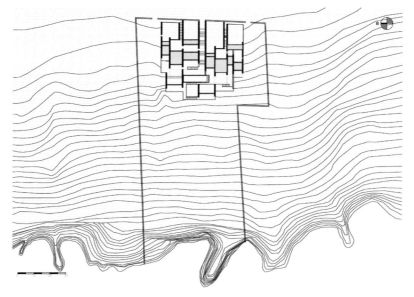

Site plan

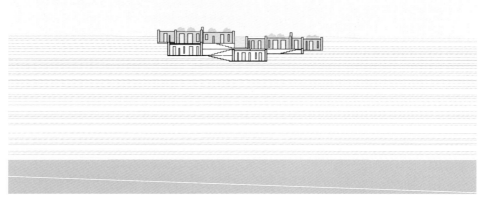

West elevation

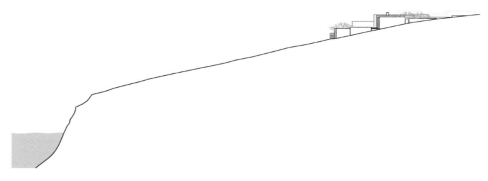

South elevation

This residential complex leaves the natural landscape intact and is perfectly suited to the sloping terrain, leaving the east side practically buried.

La création du complexe résidentiel laisse intact le paysage naturel et s'adapte parfaitement au terrain en pente, de manière que le côté est se trouve pratiquement sous terre.

Die Schaffung des Wohnkomplexes lässt die natürliche Landschaft intakt und adaptiert sich perfekt an die Hanglage des Grundstücks, so dass die Ostseite praktisch unterirdisch liegt.

La creación del complejo residencial deja intacto el paisaje natural y se adapta perfectamente a la pendiente del terreno, de modo que el lado este se encuentra prácticamente enterrado.

The interior and exterior walls are made from the archetypal material of the Cyclades, sometimes acting as a boundary and sometimes as an element of the house itself.

Les murs et les enceintes sont réalisés suivant la forme archétypale des îles Cyclades, qui est parfois utilisée comme une limite ou comme un élément de la maison.

Wände und Mauern sind in der für die Kykladen-Inseln archetypischen Form umgesetzt, wo sie manchmal als Begrenzung und dann wieder als Wohnelement verwendet werden.

Las paredes y muros se realizan con la forma arquetípica de las islas Cícladas, donde unas veces se utiliza como límite y otras como un elemento de la vivienda.

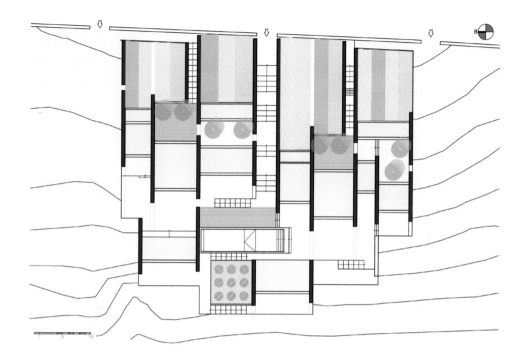

Roof floor plan

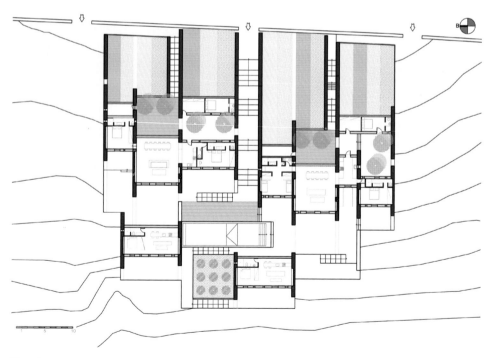

Floor plan

RIVER HOUSE

Mark Dziewulski Architect
Carmichael, California, United States
© Keith Cronin

The spectacular design of this house is a response to its natural context: a soft, wooded hillside overlooking the river and the natural park on the opposite bank. Thus, the result of Mark Dziewoulski's work is a dynamic sculptural form that floats over the ground and tells a story, without pause but without haste, of the journey from public space to private sanctuary.

La conception spectaculaire de la maison répond au contexte naturel : une pente douce et boisée donnant sur la rivière et le parc naturel de la rive opposée. Ainsi, le résultat du travail de Mark Dziewoulski est une forme dynamique et sculpturale qui flotte sur le terrain, qui décrit, sans s'arrêter mais sans hâte, un voyage de ce qui est du domaine public au sanctuaire du domaine privé.

Das spektakuläre Design dieses Wohnhauses ist eine Antwort auf den natürlichen Kontext: Ein leichter und bewaldeter Hang mit Blick auf den Fluss und den Naturpark am gegenüberliegenden Ufer. Auf diese Weise ist das Ergebnis der Arbeit von Mark Dziewoulski eine dynamische und bildhauerische Form, die über dem Boden schwebt, die pausenlos aber ohne Eile eine Reise vom Öffentlichen ins Allerheiligste des Privaten beschreibt.

El espectacular diseño de la vivienda es una respuesta al contexto natural: una pendiente suave y arbolada con vistas al río y al parque natural de la orilla opuesta. De esta forma, el resultado del trabajo de Mark Dziewoulski es una forma dinámica y escultórica que flota sobre el terreno, que describe, sin pausa pero sin prisas, un viaje desde lo público hasta el santuario de lo privado.

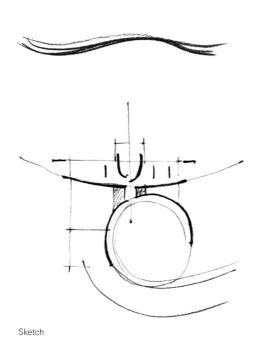

Sketch

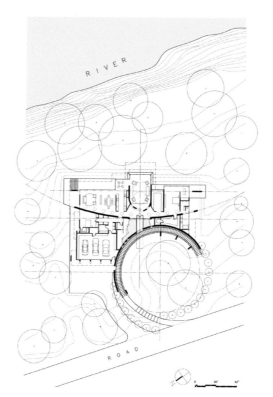

Site plan

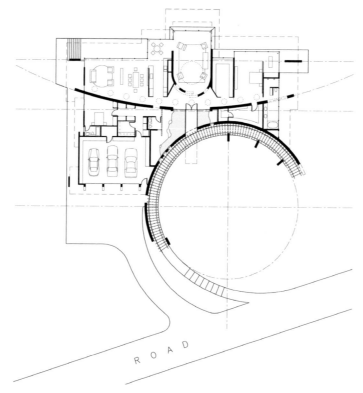

Floor plan

The high continuous glass wall, protected under the long overhanging eaves, is a unique wildlife observatory.

Le grand mur continu en verre, protégé par de longs auvents saillants, est un observatoire unique sur la faune sauvage.

Die hohe durchgängige Glaswand, die von langen Dachüberständen geschützt wird, ist ein unvergleichliches Observatorium der wildlebenden Tiere und Pflanzen.

La alta pared continua de vidrio, protegida bajo largos aleros voladizos, es un inigualable observatorio de la vida silvestre.

The entrance, via a bridge over a koi pond, introduces a water theme: its sight and sound represent a transition from public to private, from manmade to natural.

L'entrée, via un pont sur un étang *koi*, fait de l'eau son thème principal : la vision et le son de l'eau font la transition de ce qui est du domaine public de ce qui est du domaine privé, de ce qui a été construit par l'homme et de ce qui est naturel.

Den Eingang bildet eine über einen Koi-Teich führende Brücke, sie führt das Wasser als Thema ein: Sein Anblick und sein Klang repräsentieren den Übergang vom Öffentlichen zum Privaten beziehungsweise über den Menschen zur Natur.

La entrada, a través de un puente sobre un estanque *koi*, introduce el agua como tema: su visión y su sonido representan la transición de público a privado, de lo hecho por el hombre a lo natural.

The house's design retained as many mature trees as possible, to act as sun filters and enhance the concept of life in nature.

La conception de la maison préserve le plus grand nombre d'arbres anciens possible, qui agissent comme des filtres solaires et améliorent davantage le concept de vie dans la nature.

Der Entwurf des Wohnhauses erhält die höchstmögliche Anzahl an großen Bäumen, die als Sonnenfilter dienen und zudem dem Konzept des Lebens in der Natur zuträglich sind.

El diseño de la vivienda preserva el mayor número de árboles maduros posible, que actúan como filtros solares y mejoran aún más el concepto de vida en la naturaleza.

PORT LUDLOW RESIDENCE

FINNE Architects
Puget Sound, Washington, United States
© Benjamin Benschneider

This design by FINNE Architects is a modern and compact house located on a wooded seafront plot in the extreme north of the Hood Canal, a long peninsula, like a fjord, in the west of Puget Sound. The property is largely composed of a simple glazed space, which opens completely to become a gateway to the beauty of its natural surroundings.

La conception de FINNE Architects est une maison moderne et compacte située sur une propriété boisée face à la mer, à l'extrême nord du canal de Hood; un bras de canal long comme un fjord, à l'ouest de Puget Sound. La maison est composée en grande partie d'un espace vitré simple qui s'ouvre entièrement pour devenir la porte qui donne sur la beauté de son environnement naturel.

Dieser Entwurf von FINNE Architects ist ein modernes und sehr kompaktes Wohnhaus, auf einem bewaldeten Wassergrundstück am nördlichen Ende des Hood Canals, eines langen fjordähnlichen Seitenarms westlich von Puget Sound. Das Wohnhaus besteht zum großen Teil aus einem einfachen verglasten Teil, der sich komplett öffnet, um sich in ein Eintrittstor für die Schönheit der umgebenden Natur zu verwandeln.

El diseño de FINNE Architects es una vivienda moderna y muy compacta situada en una propiedad arbolada frente al mar, en el extremo norte del canal de Hood; un brazo largo, como un fiordo, del oeste de Puget Sound. La vivienda está en gran parte compuesta por un sencillo espacio acristalado que se abre por completo para convertirse en una puerta de entrada a la belleza de su entorno natural.

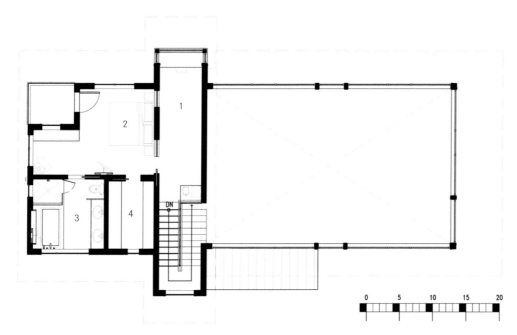

Second floor plan

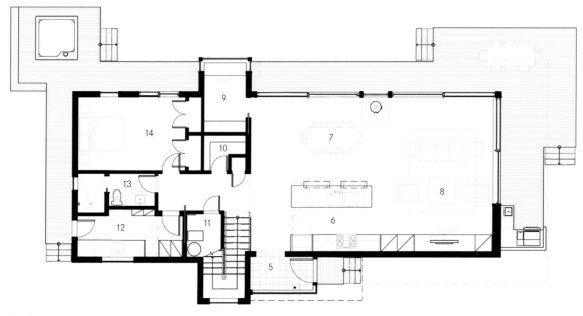

Main floor plan

1. Study
2. Master bedroom
3. Master bathroom
4. Master closet
5. Entrance
6. Kitchen
7. Dining room
8. Living room
9. Office
10. Pantry
11. Mechanical room
12. Laundry
13. Bathroom
14. Guest room

The main section of the lounge is fully glazed. 12-foot high glass walls open to slightly elevated wooden deck and stunning views over the sea.

Le volume principal du salon est entièrement vitré. Des murs en verre d'une hauteur de 3,65 mètres s'ouvrent sur une terrasse en bois légèrement surélevée et sur d'impressionnantes vues sur la mer.

Der Hauptteil des Wohnraums ist vollständig verglast. Etwa 3,65 Meter hohe Glaswände öffnen sich einer leicht erhöhten Holzterrasse und den beeindruckenden Blicken über das Wasser.

El volumen principal del salón está completamente acristalado. Muros de cristal de 3,65 metros de alto se abren a una terraza de madera ligeramente elevada y a las impresionantes vistas sobre el mar.

The interior finishes are simple and elegant: ipe wood floors, kitchen cupboard doors in zebrawood with mahogany panelling at the ends, and quartz and limestone worktops.

Les finitions intérieures sont simples et élégantes : des sols en bois d'ipé, des portes d'armoires de cuisine en bois de zèbre et des panneaux en acajou aux extrémités, ainsi que des plans de travail en quartz et en pierre calcaire.

Die Verarbeitungen im Inneren sind einfach und elegant: Böden aus Ipé-Holz, Küchenschranktüren aus Zebrano-Holz, Paneele aus Mahagoni an den Seiten und Arbeitsplatten aus Quarz und Kalkstein.

Los acabados interiores son sencillos y elegantes: suelos de madera de ipé, puertas de armario de cocina de zebrano y paneles de caoba en los extremos, y encimeras de cuarzo y piedra caliza.

FIDAR HOUSE

Raëd Abillama, Géraldine Bruneel
Fidar, Jbeil, Lebanon
© Géraldine Bruneel

Located on the north coast of Lebanon, this project by Raed Abillama Architects manages to preserve the natural qualities of the area, thanks mainly to its seamless integration with the existing landscape. Despite the rugged nature of the terrain, the smart design allows the house to sit on a relatively flat plane between a private road and the nearby coastline.

Le projet de Raëd Abillama Architects, situé sur la côte nord du Liban, parvient à préserver les qualités naturelles du lieu, grâce, principalement, à son intégration parfaite dans le paysage existant. Malgré la nature accidentée du terrain, la conception intelligente du projet permet de construire la maison sur un site relativement plat, entre un chemin privé et le littoral proche.

Dem Projekt von Raëd Abillama Architects, an der Nordküste Libanons gelegen, gelingt es, die natürlichen Qualitäten des Ortes zu erhalten, vor allem dank der perfekten Integration in die vorhandene Landschaft. Trotz der rauen Umgebung ermöglicht es der intelligente Entwurf, das Wohnhaus auf einem relativ ebenen Bereich zu platzieren, zwischen einem Privatweg und der nahe gelegenen Küstenlinie.

El proyecto de Raëd Abillama Architects, situado en la costa norte del Líbano, consigue preservar las cualidades naturales del lugar, gracias, sobre todo, a la perfecta integración con el paisaje existente. Pese a la naturaleza agreste del terreno, el inteligente diseño permite asentar la vivienda en una área relativamente plana, entre un camino privado y la cercana línea de costa.

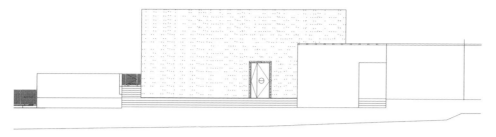

Elevation A

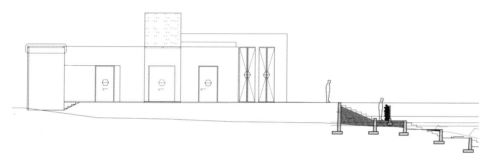

Elevation C

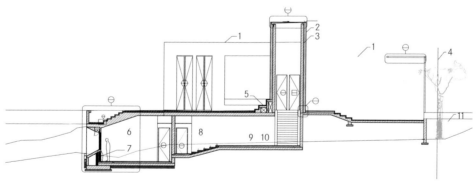

Section A

1. Plaster and paint finish
2. Stone cladding cut at random sizes horizontally united
3. Concrete wall
4. Set back limit
5. Concrete bench
6. Rolling shutter
7. Heater in recess below window
8. Screed
9. 5 cm screed
10. 8 cm backfill
11. Planter for trees
12. Stone cladding
13. Shaft
14. Opening for fan
15. Steps: fairfaced smooth concrete appearance
16. For all staircases (inside and outside): the steps must be of fairfaced smooth concrete. On section D and everywhere where the terrace of the GF is the roof of the basement we have to add 3-4 cm foam. The finishing levels must not be changed

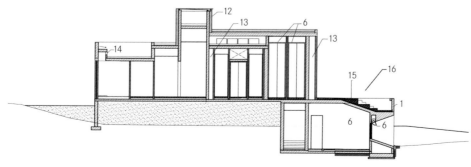

Section D

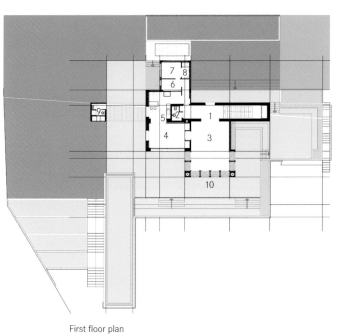

First floor plan

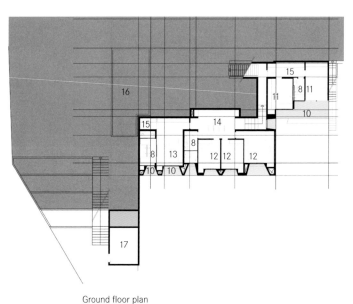

Ground floor plan

1. Entrance
2. Toilet
3. Main living room
4. Dining room
5. Kitchen
6. Laundry
7. Service room
8. Bathroom
9. Outdoor toilet/ Showers
10. Terrace
11. Guest bedroom
12. Bedroom
13. Master bedroom
14. Living room
15. Closet space
16. Water tank
17. Mechanical room

Facing towards the coast, the infinity pool provides an unparalleled sense of continuity and connection with the Mediterranean.

La piscine, aux bords infinis et orientée en direction de la côte, procure une sensation de continuité et de communion inégalable avec la Mer Méditerranée.

Der zur Küste ausgerichtete Infinity Pool vermittelt ein unvergleichliches Gefühl der Fortsetzung im und der Verbundenheit mit dem Mittelmeer.

La piscina, de borde infinito y orientada hacia la costa, proporciona una inigualable sensación de continuidad y de unión con el mar Mediterráneo.

Built as an elevated platform on low columns, the upper level minimises the disruption of the natural rocky landscape, whilst at the same time enhancing the views of the coast.

L'étage supérieur, construit comme une plate-forme surélevée sur des colonnes basses, n'altère pas le paysage rocheux naturel, et permet en même temps d'avoir une vue sur la côte.

Die als Plattform auf niedrigen Säulen konstruierte obere Ebene minimiert die Veränderung der natürlichen Felslandschaft und verbessert zugleich den Ausblick auf die Küste.

El nivel superior, construido como una plataforma elevada sobre columnas bajas, minimiza la alteración del paisaje rocoso natural, al tiempo que mejora las vistas de la costa.

SURF HOUSE

Max Pritchard Architect
Adelaide, South Australia, Australia
© Sam Noonan

The extensive use of stone and wood reflects the owners' passion for 1950s and 1960s architecture. Their other great passion, surfing, is responsible for the house's particular location, on a plot with direct access to and stunning views over a famous Australian surf beach. Max Prichard's work certainly brought his clients' dreams to life.

L'utilisation massive de la pierre et du bois reflète la passion des propriétaires pour l'architecture des années 50 et 60. Leur autre grande passion, le surf, est la raison pour laquelle la maison se trouve à cet endroit en particulier : un terrain avec un accès et de magnifiques vues sur une célèbre plage de surf australienne. Sans aucun doute, le travail de Max Prichard peut matérialiser le rêve de ses clients.

Die großzügige Verwendung von Stein und Holz spiegelt die Leidenschaft der Eigentümer für die Architektur der 50er und 60er Jahre wider. Ihre andere große Passion, das Surfen, ist der Grund dafür, dass sich das Haus an genau diesem Ort befindet: Auf einem Grundstück mit Zugang zu und wunderschönen Blicken auf einen berühmten australischen Surfstrand. Ohne Zweifel gelingt es der Arbeit von Max Prichard, die Träume seiner Auftraggeber wahr werden zu lassen.

El uso extensivo de la piedra y la madera refleja la pasión de los propietarios por la arquitectura de los años 50 y 60. Su otra gran pasión, el surf, es la causante de que la vivienda se encuentre en esa ubicación en particular: un terreno con acceso y hermosas vistas a una famosa playa australiana de surf. Sin duda, el trabajo de Max Prichard logra materializar el sueño de sus clientes.

On the ground floor, an intimate lounge at ground level, with a curved sofa and a wood-burning stove, contrasts with the upper level that is completely open to the outside.

Au rez-de-chaussée, un salon intime au niveau du sol, avec un canapé arrondi et un poêle à bois contrastent avec l'étage supérieur entièrement ouvert sur l'extérieur.

Im unteren Geschoss bildet ein intimes ebenerdiges Wohnzimmer mit einem kurvigen Sofa und einem Holzofen einen Kontrast zum vollständig nach außen offenen Obergeschoss.

En la planta baja, una íntima sala de estar a ras de suelo, con un sofá curvo y una estufa de leña contrastan con el nivel superior completamente abierto al exterior.

LAKE LUGANO HOUSE

JM Architecture, architect Jacopo Mascheroni
Lugano, Switzerland
© Jacopo Mascheroni

Seated on the slope of a hill near the shore of Lake Lugano, This house is made up of two structures that are set at different levels due to the specific characteristics of the terrain. The upper section, a glass polygon pavilion with rounded edges, is definitely the space that draws attention to JM Architecture.

Située sur la pente d'une colline proche de la rive du lac Lugano, la maison est formée de deux volumes qui, en raison des caractéristiques particulières du terrain, se structurent en différents niveaux. Le volume supérieur, un pavillon en verre de forme polygonale et aux extrémités arrondies est, certainement, l'espace qui attire tous les regards de la conception de JM Architecture.

Am Hang eines Hügels in der Nähe vom Rande des Luganer Sees bilden zwei Räume das Wohnhaus, welche aufgrund der besonderen Geländegegebenheiten auf unterschiedlichen Ebenen liegen. Die obere Ebene, ein polygonaler Glaspavillon mit runden Ecken, ist zweifelsohne der Raum, der alle Blicke auf den Entwurf von JM Architecture zieht.

Asentada en la pendiente de una colina cercana a la costa del lago Lugano, la vivienda la componen dos volúmenes que, a causa de las particulares características del terreno, se organizan en niveles diferentes. El volumen superior, un pabellón de cristal de forma poligonal y bordes redondeados es, sin duda, el espacio que atrae todas las miradas sobre el diseño de JM Architecture.

Upper level

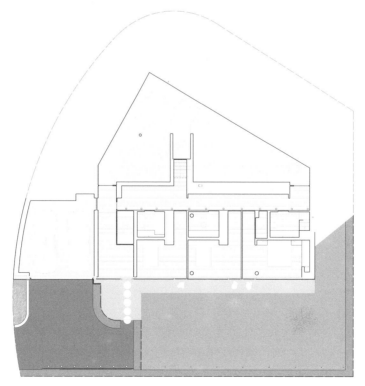

Lower level

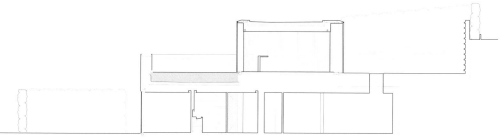

Section

The space between the perimeter wall and pavilion provides constant ventilation and natural light in the living areas. The white coating of the walls and the white gravel reflect the sunlight.

L'espace entre le mur d'enceinte et le pavillon facilite l'aération constante et la lumière naturelle dans les parties communes. Le revêtement blanc du mur et le gravier blanc reflètent la lumière du soleil.

Der Raum zwischen der umgebenden Mauer und dem Pavillon ermöglicht konstante Ventilation und natürliches Licht in den Aufenthaltsbereichen. Das Weiß der Mauer und der weiße Kies reflektieren das Sonnenlicht.

El espacio entre el muro perimetral y el pabellón facilita la ventilación constante y luz natural en las zonas de estar. El revestimiento blanco del muro y la grava blanca reflejan la luz del sol.

The glass pavilion has two distinct areas with well-defined views, looking to the mountains from the most private parts of the pavilion and to the garden and lake from the living area.

Le pavillon en verre possède deux zones distinctes avec des vues bien définies : vers la montagne, pour la partie la plus privée du pavillon, et vers le jardin avec une vue sur le lac pour les parties communes.

Der Glaspavillon verfügt über zwei differenzierte Bereiche mit gut definierten Ausblicken: Auf die Berge im privateren Bereich des Pavillons und auf den Garten mit Blick auf den See im Wohnbereich.

El pabellón de cristal cuenta con dos áreas diferenciadas con vistas bien definidas: hacia la montaña, en la parte más privada del pabellón, y hacia el jardín con vistas al lago en la zona de vida.

CLEAR LAKE COTTAGE

MacLennan Jaunkalns Miller Architects (MJMA)
Township of Sequin, Ontario, Canada
© Ben Rahn, © A Frame Photography

With their renovation of this 1950s house, MJMA achieved their objective of capturing the rural qualities of this Clear Lake community. Its design provides a clean and modern ambience, which also sits easily within the natural landscape that surrounds it and captures the beautiful country cottage feel that the owners so desired.

L'objectif que MJMA atteint en rénovant cette maison de 1950 est de saisir le caractère rural qui règne dans la communauté tranquille du lac Clear. Elle est conçue pour profiter d'un environnement propre et moderne qui, de plus, s'intègre facilement au paysage naturel environnant tout en donnant une jolie sensation de "maison de campagne" que les propriétaires souhaitaient vraiment.

Das Ziel, welches MJMA mit der Sanierung dieses Wohnhauses von 1950 erreicht, ist es, den ruralen Charakter, den man in der ruhigen Gemeinde am Clear Lake spürt, einzufangen. Sein Entwurf ermöglicht es, ein sauberes und modernes Umfeld zu genießen, zudem gelingt es ihm, sich leicht in die umgebende natürliche Landschaft einzufügen und zugleich ein wunderbares „Landhaus"-Gefühl einzufangen, welches sich seine Eigentümer so sehr wünschten.

El objetivo que MJMA logra con la renovación de esta vivienda de 1950 es captar el carácter rural que se respira en la tranquila comunidad del lago Clear. Su diseño permite disfrutar de un ambiente limpio y moderno que, además, consigue acoplarse con facilidad al paisaje natural circundante y, a la vez, capturar una hermosa sensación de "casa de campo" que sus propietarios tanto deseaban.

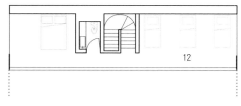

Upper floor plan

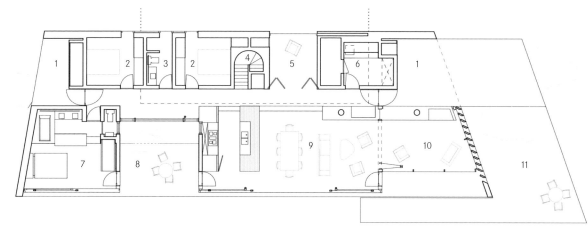

Ground floor plan

1. Entrance
2. Bedroom
3. Toilet
4. Stairs
5. Paul's room
6. Utility/Mud room
7. Master bedroom
8. Morning terrace
9. Kitchen/Dining/Living
10. Screened porch
11. Day terrace
12. Upper loft

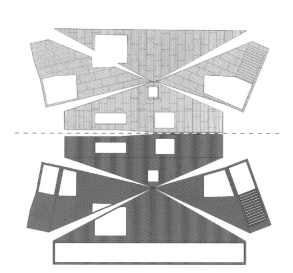

Unfolded skin

Diagram of roof

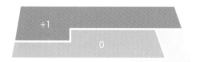

Levels

Indoor/Outdoor

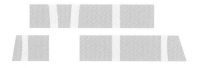

Cross ventilation

Diagrams of sustainability

Ceiling and walls merge into one unique structure, drawing the open-air spaces into the interior and thus creating a continuum between inside and out.

Le toit et les murs se fondent dans une même structure unique. De cette façon, elle réussit à attirer vers l'intérieur les espaces à l'air libre, avec un espace continu entre l'intérieur et l'extérieur.

Dach und Wände verschmelzen zu einer einzigen Struktur. Auf diese Weise gelingt es, die äußeren Räume nach innen zu holen durch einen durchgehenden Raum zwischen Innen und Außen.

Techo y paredes se funden en una misma estructura singular. De esta forma, logra captar hacia el interior los espacios al aire libre, con un continuo espacial entre el interior y el exterior.

The roof is designed like a tent, with a single pole supporting the cover and a hipped roof—an innovative way of defining the inner sections.

Le plafond est conçu comme une tente : un pilier unique soutient la toiture à quatre pentes et délimite les volumes intérieurs de façon originale.

Das Dach ist wie das eines Zeltes entworfen: Ein einziger Balken hält die Dachhaut, lässt sie in vier Richtungen abfallen und definiert die Innenräume auf originelle Art und Weise.

El techo está diseñado como el de una tienda de campaña: un único poste sostiene la cubierta, la configura a cuatro aguas y define los volúmenes interiores de forma original.

LUJAN HOUSE

Robert M. Gurney, FAIA, Architect
Ocean View, Delaware, United States
© Hoachlander Davis Photography

The Quillen's Point neighbourhood, near the Chesapeake Bay in Ocean View, is comprised of modest houses on small plots. It is an eclectic mix of homes, gravel roads and forest areas, creating a nostalgic and informal atmosphere. Robert M. Gurney's house design manages to balance the picturesque landscape and an intimate and secluded atmosphere in the garden.

Le quartier de Quillen's Point, près de la baie de Chesapeake à Ocean View, est formé de maisons modestes sur de petites parcelles. C'est un mélange éclectique de maisons, de chemins en gravier et de zones boisées qui offre une atmosphère nostalgique et informelle. La conception de la maison de Robert M. Gurney parvient à trouver un équilibre entre un paysage pittoresque et une ambiance de jardin intime et isolé.

Das Viertel Quillen's Point an der Chesapeake Bay in Ocean View besteht aus bescheidenen Häusern in kleinen Parzellen. Es ist eine eklektische Mischung aus Häusern, Kieswegen und Waldstücken, die ein nostalgisches und informales Gefühl vermittelt. Dem Entwurf des Wohnhauses von Robert M. Gurney gelingt es, ein Gleichgewicht zwischen der pittoresken Landschaft und einem trauten und abgeschiedenen Gartenambiente zu schaffen.

El barrio de Quillen's Point, junto a la bahía de Chesapeake en Ocean View, está compuesto por casas modestas en pequeñas parcelas. Es una mezcla ecléctica de casas, caminos de grava y áreas boscosas que proporciona un ambiente nostálgico e informal. El diseño de la vivienda de Robert M. Gurney logra establecer un equilibrio entre el paisaje pintoresco y un ambiente de jardín íntimo y aislado.

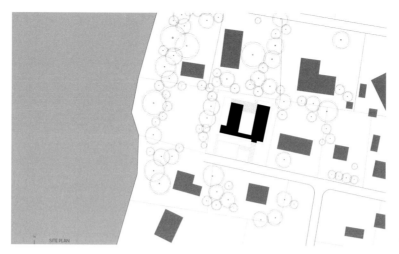

Site plan

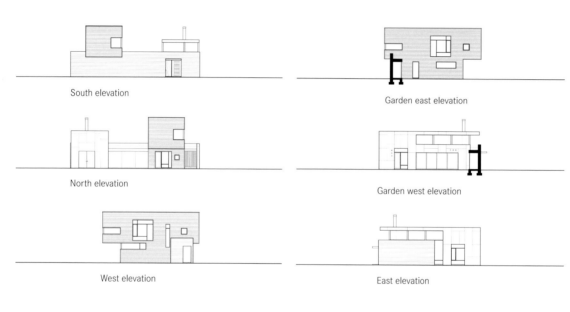

South elevation

Garden east elevation

North elevation

Garden west elevation

West elevation

East elevation

Axonometric views

Garden east section

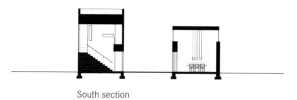

South section

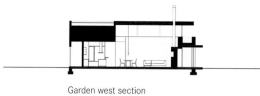

Garden west section

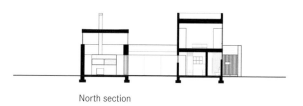

North section

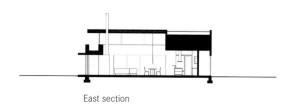

East section

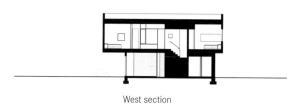

West section

First floor plan

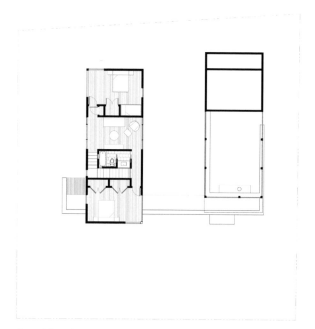

Second floor plan

The house is conceived in two simple flat-roofed structures of different heights that intersect and overlap with a one-storey space connecting them.

La maison est conçue en deux volumes simples, au toit plat, dont la hauteur varie et qui se croisent et se superposent avec un espace en hauteur pour circuler, qui les relie.

Das Wohnhaus ist als zwei einfache Blöcke mit geradem Dach konzipiert, die sich in der Höhe unterscheiden und sich kreuzen und überlagern, mit einem einstöckigen Raum, der sie verbindet.

La vivienda está concebida en dos volúmenes simples, de techo plano, que varían en altura y que se cruzan y se superponen con un espacio de circulación, de un piso de altura, que los conecta.

The design has endeavoured to integrate the living spaces with the open air via a central garden, whilst retaining privacy in relation to the neighbouring houses.

La conception s'est efforcée d'intégrer les parties communes dans l'espace en plein air à partir d'un jardin central, tout en maintenant l'intimité des maisons voisines.

Bei dem Entwurf ging es darum, die Wohnräume in den von einem zentralen Garten ausgehenden Außenraum zu integrieren und gleichzeitig die Privatsphäre im Hinblick auf die benachbarten Häuser zu erhalten.

El diseño se ha esforzado por integrar los espacios de vida en el espacio al aire libre a partir de un jardín central, mientras se mantiene la privacidad respecto a las casas vecinas.

OAK PASS GUEST

Walker Workshop
Beverly Hills, California, United States
© Nicholas Alan Cope
www.cope1.com

This Walker Workshop Design Build project is a two-bedroomed guesthouse with enough space to accommodate an entire family. However, situated on a ridge in a forest of tall trees, the house needs little space and height to maximise the panoramic views to the nearby canyon, while also establishing a close connection with the trees that are nearest to it.

Le projet de Walker Workshop Design Build est une maison d'hôtes avec deux chambres et une capacité suffisante pour accueillir toute une famille. Cependant, la maison, située sur la crête d'une forêt de grands arbres, nécessite peu d'espace et de hauteur pour optimiser les vues panoramiques sur le canyon qui se trouve à proximité, tout en établissant un lien étroit avec les arbres les plus proches.

Das Projekt von Walker Workshop Design Build ist ein Gästehaus mit zwei Schlafzimmern und mit ausreichend Kapazität, eine ganze Familie aufzunehmen. Allerdings benötigt das auf dem Kamm eines Waldes mit hohen Bäumen gelegene Haus wenig Raum und Höhe, um den Panoramablick auf die nahe gelegene Schlucht zu maximieren, zugleich bildet es eine enge Verbindung zu den nächst gelegenen Bäumen.

El proyecto de Walker Workshop Design Build es una casa de invitados de dos habitaciones, con la capacidad suficiente como para acoger a toda una familia. Sin embargo, situada en una cresta de un bosque de altos árboles, la vivienda necesita poco espacio y altura para maximizar la vistas panorámicas al cercano cañón, a la vez que establece una estrecha conexión con los árboles más cercanos.

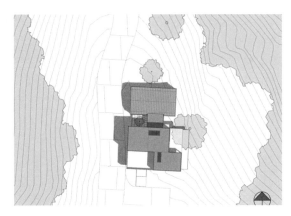

Site plan

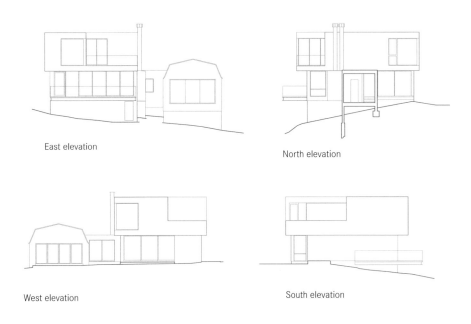

East elevation

North elevation

West elevation

South elevation

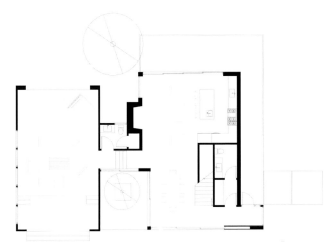

First floor plan

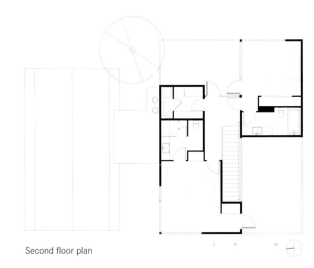

Second floor plan

On the upper floor, which is completely clad in fire-resistant wood, the rooms are located in opposite corners of the floating shape.

Au premier étage, entièrement recouvert de bois résistant au feu, les chambres sont situées aux extrémités du volume flottant.

Im oberen Stockwerk, das vollständig mit feuerbeständigem Holz verschalt ist, liegen die Zimmer in den gegenüberliegenden Ecken des schwimmenden Baukörpers.

En la planta superior, totalmente revestida de madera resistente al fuego, las habitaciones están situadas en las esquinas opuestas del volumen flotante.

HOLY CROSS

T B A / Thomas Balaban Architecte
Montreal, Quebec, Canada
© Adrien Williams

This 300 m² detached house hides a rich spatial complexity behind its tough working-class façade. Thomas Balaban took an old house in a typical post-war neighbourhood as his starting point and adapted it to its surroundings, succeeding in making it stand out in a heterogeneous context without resorting to mimicry or compromising the project's contemporaneity.

Les 300 m² de cette maison individuelle cachent une complexité spatiale riche derrière sa façade austère de classe ouvrière. Thomas Balaban prend comme point de départ une vieille maison d'un quartier typique d'après-guerre et parvient, tout en l'adaptant à l'environnement, à la rendre unique dans un contexte hétérogène, sans avoir recours au mimétisme et sans renoncer à l'aspect contemporain du projet.

Die 300 m² dieses Einfamilienhauses verbergen eine reiche räumliche Komplexität hinter ihrer harten Arbeiterklassen-Fassade. Thomas Balaban nimmt als Ausgangspunkt ein altes Haus aus einem typischen Nachkriegsviertel und schafft es, sich zwar an die Umgebung anzupassen, aber innerhalb eines heterogenen Kontextes herauszuragen, ungekünstelt und ohne Abstriche an der Aktualität des Projekts.

Los 300 m² de esta vivienda unifamiliar esconden una rica complejidad espacial detrás de su dura fachada de clase obrera. Thomas Balaban toma como punto de partida una vieja casa de un típico barrio de posguerra y consigue que, al mismo tiempo que se adapta a su entorno, destaque dentro un contexto heterogéneo, sin recurrir a la mímica y sin renunciar a la contemporaneidad del proyecto.

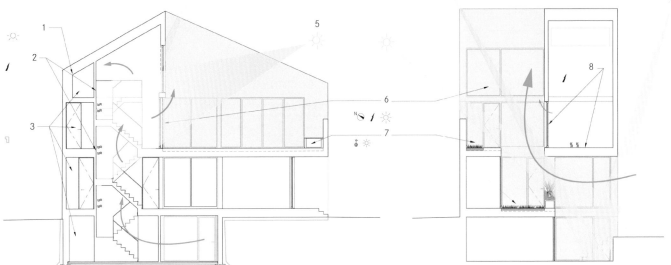

1. Operable window
2. Concrete wall
3. Bathrooms and storage
4. Summer sun diffused by interior shades
5. Direct solar gain for passive solar heating in winter
6. Large windows on the south façade
7. Terrace with garden
8. Concrete floor and glazed openings

a. Orientation
The house is oriented to maximise sun exposure from the south and minimise heat loos to the north.

b. Light and natural ventilation
The stepped terraces and central interior court allow natural light to permeate each floor. The large glazed south wall in combination with the open stair not only increases access to natural light within the house but allows for natural ventilation to move through each floor. During the summer, shades are used to prevent the penetration of direct sun and to provide bioclimatic comfort.

c. Organization
The bathrooms and storage areas are place on the north side of the house while the living spaces surround the central courtyard and terrace to maximise access to natural light.

d. Passive energy
Passive thermal gain is obtained by combining large windows on the south and west façades with concrete floors and partition wall.

e. Terraces and gardens
Planting on the terraces reinforces the vision of a sustainable environment and aids in the creation of a microclimate.

f. Construction
A prefabricated high performance timber-framed wall system is used for an efficient use of material and to minimise waste related to the construction process. This strategy allows for a higher level of productivity, and greater energy-efficiency.

Diagrams of sustainable strategies

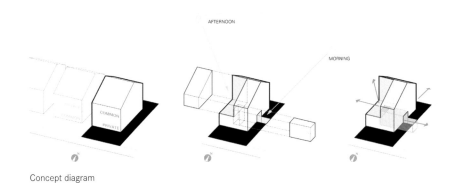

Concept diagram

Outside, the house is contained, light and monochromatic, emphasising the general morphology of its details.

À l'extérieur, la maison est contenue, légère et monochromatique, ce qui permet de souligner la morphologie générale des détails.

Außen ist das Haus zurückhaltend, leicht und monochromatisch, wodurch die allgemeine Morphologie mehr Gewicht bekommt als die Details.

En el exterior, la casa es contenida, ligera y monocromática, lo cual permite enfatizar la morfología general sobre los detalles.

The light in the centre is drawn down into the heart of the house. By bringing the living spaces to the upper level, he has maximised the direct sunlight where it is most needed.

La lumière disponible en son centre est attirée vers le bas dans le cœur de la maison. En réunissant les parties communes à l'étage, la lumière directe du soleil est optimisée là où elle est le plus nécessaire.

Das in der Mitte verfügbare Licht zeichnet sich nach unten bis ins Herz des Hauses ab. Durch die Verbindung der Wohnräume im oberen Teil wird das direkte Sonnenlicht da maximiert, wo es am meisten gebraucht wird.

La luz disponible en el centro se dibuja hacia abajo en el corazón de la casa. Al reunir los espacios de vida en la parte superior, se maximiza la luz solar directa donde más se necesita.

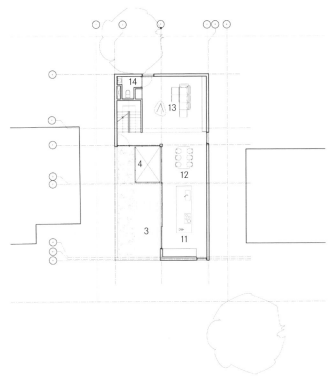

First level floor plan

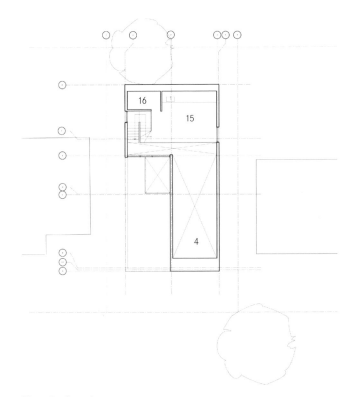

Mezzanine floor plan

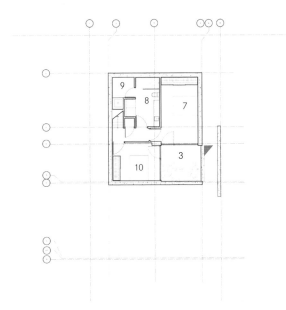

Lower level floor plan

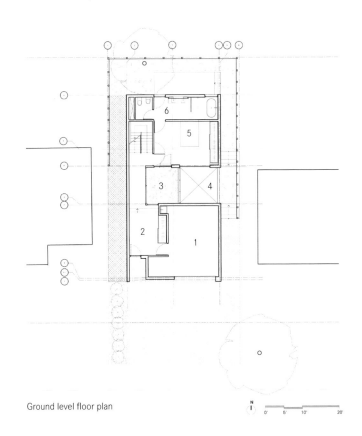

Ground level floor plan

1. Parking
2. Entrance
3. Garden/Terrace
4. Open to below
5. Master bedroom
6. Master bathroom
7. Bedroom
8. Bathroom/Laundry
9. Mechanical room
10. Guest bedroom
11. Kitchen
12. Dining room
13. Living room
14. Toilet
15. Mezzanine/Study
16. Storage room

STEELHOUSE 1+2

Zack | de Vito Architecture
San Francisco, California, United States
© Paul Dyer Photography

Vacant plots for new-build houses are rarely available in the heart of San Francisco. Given this phenomenal opportunity, Zack | De Vito's team squeezed the largest share out of a plot where two architects were building two different projects. The result is two urban homes, one completely new and the other based on an existing structure, set around a shared courtyard.

Des terrains libres pour développer de nouveaux projets sont rarement disponibles en plein cœur de San Francisco. Face à cette occasion incroyable, l'équipe de Zack | De Vito a tiré le meilleur parti d'un terrain où deux architectes ont développé deux projets. Il en résulte, deux maisons urbaines agencées autour d'une cour commune, l'une totalement neuve et l'autre qui profite d'une structure existante.

Freie Grundstücke zum Bau neuer Projekte sind in ganz San Francisco Mangelware. Angesichts dieser phänomenalen Chance holte das Team von Zack | De Vito das Maximum aus einem Teil des Grundstücks heraus, auf dem zwei Architekten zwei Projekte entwickelten. Das Ergebnis: Zwei städtische Wohnhäuser, eines total neu und das andere nutzte die vorhandene Substanz, beide um einen gemeinsamen Innenhof organisiert.

Parcelas vacantes donde desarrollar nuevos proyectos, rara vez están disponibles en pleno San Francisco. Ante esta fenomenal oportunidad, el equipo de Zack | De Vito extrajo el máximo partido de un terreno donde dos arquitectos desarrollaron dos proyectos. El resultado, dos viviendas urbanas, una totalmente nueva y otra que aprovecha una estructura existente, organizadas alrededor de un patio común.

East elevation

West elevation

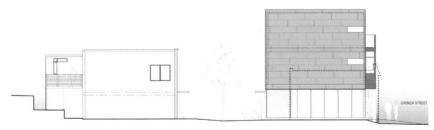

North elevation

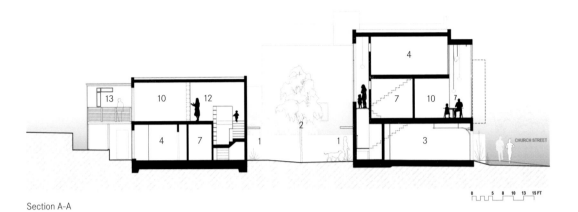

Section A-A

Ground floor plan

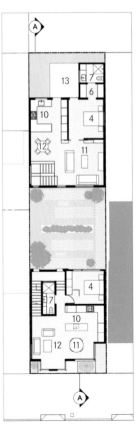

First floor plan

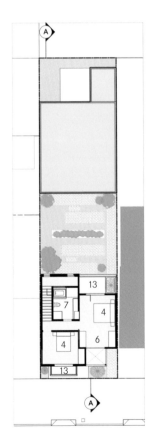

Second floor plan

1. Entrance
2. Courtyard
3. Parking
4. Bedroom
5. Study/Office
6. Walk-in wardrobe
7. Bathroom
8. Laundry
9. Mechanical room
10. Kitchen
11. Living room
12. Dining room
13. Patio/Balcony

The two houses are accessed via a shared courtyard, in contrast to a traditional street side main entrance.

Les deux maisons sont accessibles par une cour commune; en opposition à l'entrée principale traditionnelle située au niveau de la rue.

Beide Häuser sind über einen gemeinsamen Patio zugänglich und widersprechen damit dem traditionell auf der Straßenseite gelegenen Haupteingang.

Las dos viviendas son accesibles desde un patio común, en contraposición respecto a la tradicional entrada principal situada a pie de calle.

Unapologetic modern design aims to achieve maximum space efficiency, giving special attention to details and quality craftsmanship.

La conception moderne sans complexe est réalisée dans le but d'optimiser au maximum l'espace, avec une attention particulière portée sur les détails et la qualité du travail artisanal.

Das moderne Design soll vor allem der maximalen räumlichen Effizienz dienen, wobei den Details und der Qualität der handwerklichen Arbeiten besonderes Augenmerk geschenkt wurde.

El moderno diseño sin complejos está orientado a conseguir la máxima eficiencia espacial, con especial atención a los detalles y a la calidad del trabajo artesanal.

7RR ECO-HOME

Thomas Roszak Architecture
Northfield, Illinois, United States
© Thomas Roszak

The aesthetic of this house, which was designed for a newly married couple with children from a previous marriage, examines the way people live today. It experiments with the way that transparency conforms to solid shapes, eliminating boundaries and borders between inside and out so that shapes seem to 'flow in endless space.'

La conception de cette maison, prévue pour un couple de jeunes mariés ayant des enfants d'un précédent mariage, se penche sur la manière dont vivent les gens actuellement. Un projet où la transparence s'adapte aux formes solides; les frontières et les limites entre l'intérieur et l'extérieur n'existent pas, où de manière irréfutable les formes "se fondent en un espace sans fin".

Der Entwurf dieses Wohnhauses für ein frisch verheiratetes Paar mit Kindern aus einer früheren Ehe lotet die Form aus, in der diese Menschen heute leben. Ein Experiment, bei dem sich die Transparenz den festen Formen anpasst; Grenzen und Ränder zwischen Innen und Außen verschwinden, die Formen „fließen" spürbar „in einem endlosen Raum".

El diseño de esta vivienda, pensado para una pareja de recién casados con hijos de un matrimonio anterior, ahonda en la forma en que las personas viven en la actualidad. Un experimento donde la transparencia se amolda a las formas sólidas; se eliminan fronteras y bordes entre el interior y el exterior, donde de forma palpable la formas "fluyen en un espacio sin fin".

Ipe wood sun screens and shutters
block out unwanted solar rays in
summer, whilst letting in light in
the winter.

Des protections solaires en bois
d'ipé et des stores bloquent la
chaleur du soleil qui n'est pas le
bienvenu en été, mais permettent,
à la lumière d'entrer en hiver.

Sonnenschutz aus Ipé-Holz und
Jalousien verhindern im Sommer
unerwünschte Sonneneinstrahlung,
erlauben jedoch im Winter den
Eintritt von Sonnenlicht.

Protectores solares de madera
de ipé y persianas bloquean
la ganancia solar no deseada
en verano, pero permiten, sin
embargo, la entrada de luz solar
en invierno.

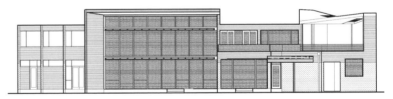

Elevations

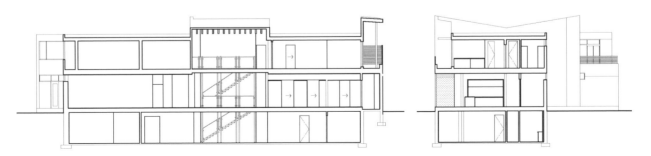

Sections

The angular design of the house is the logical response to the family's structure, building regulations, the nature of the land and the passage of the sun.

La conception angulaire de la maison est le résultat logique de la structure familiale, les règles de construction, les caractéristiques du terrain et l'orientation du soleil.

Die Winkel des Hauses ergeben sich logisch aus der Familienstruktur, den Baunormen, den Geländeeigenschaften und dem Lauf der Sonne.

El diseño angular de la vivienda es el resultado lógico de la estructura de la familia, las normas de construcción, los atributos del terreno y la trayectoria del sol.

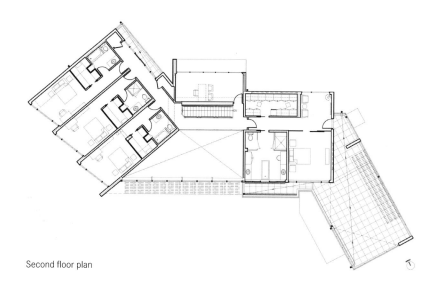

Second floor plan

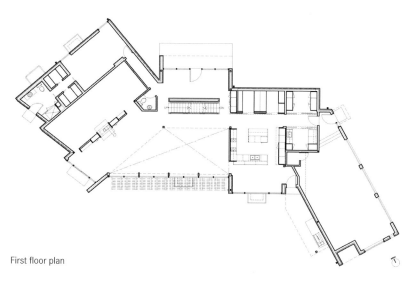

First floor plan

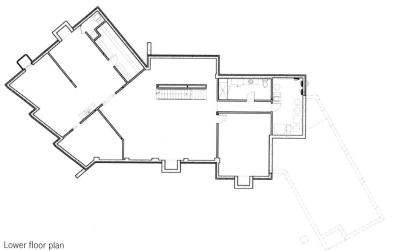

Lower floor plan

Based on square rooms and a large interstitial space for hallways, bathrooms and stairs, the design keeps the rooms pure and clear.

La conception du projet, qui repose sur des pièces carrées et un large espace interstitiel pour les couloirs, les salles de bain et les escaliers, donne aux pièces un aspect pur et clair.

Durch die Planung, die auf quadratischen Zimmern und einem großen Zwischenraum für Flure, Bäder und Treppen basiert, bleiben die Räume klar und frei.

La planificación del diseño, basada en habitaciones cuadradas y un amplio espacio intersticial para pasillos, baños y escaleras, mantiene las habitaciones puras y despejadas.

HOUSE OF TERRACES

Studio Arte
Carvoeiro, Portugal
© Luis da Cruz

The major objective of Studio Arte was to transform a simple holiday home into a family house with all the features of contemporary lifestyle. The core strategy in this renovation project focused on retaining the utmost respect for the essence of the original with its organic, pure and white construction, whilst being consistent with the premises of contemporary architecture.

L'objectif fondamental de Studio Arte a été de transformer une maison de vacances modeste en une maison familiale ayant toutes les caractéristiques de la vie contemporaine. La principale stratégie dans ce projet de rénovation a été de respecter au maximum l'essence de la construction originale – organique, pure et blanche –, et en accord avec les bases de l'architecture contemporaine.

Das große Ziel von Studio Arte war es, ein einfaches Ferienhaus in ein Wohnhaus für eine Familie mit allen Eigenschaften des zeitgemäßen Lebensstils zu verwandeln. Die Hauptstrategie bei diesem Sanierungsvorhaben konzentrierte sich auf maximalen Respekt vor der vorhandenen Bausubstanz – organisch, puristisch und weiß – und ist im Einklang mit den Prämissen der zeitgenössischen Architektur.

El gran objetivo de Studio Arte fue transformar una sencilla casa de vacaciones en una casa familiar con todas las características del estilo de vida contemporáneo. La estrategia principal en este proyecto de renovación se centró en el respeto máximo a la esencia de la construcción original —orgánica, pura y blanca—, y acorde con las premisas de la arquitectura contemporánea.

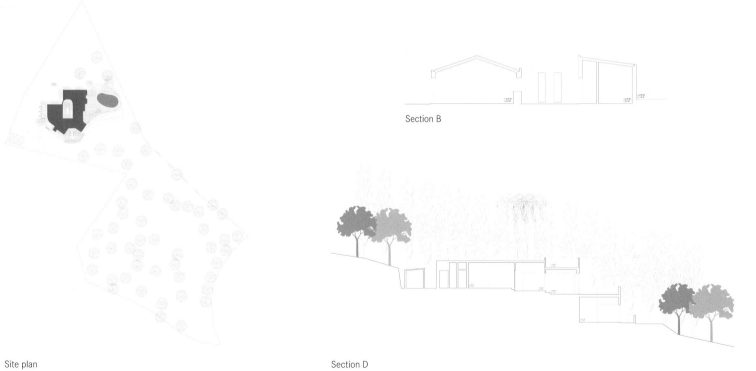

Site plan

Section B

Section D

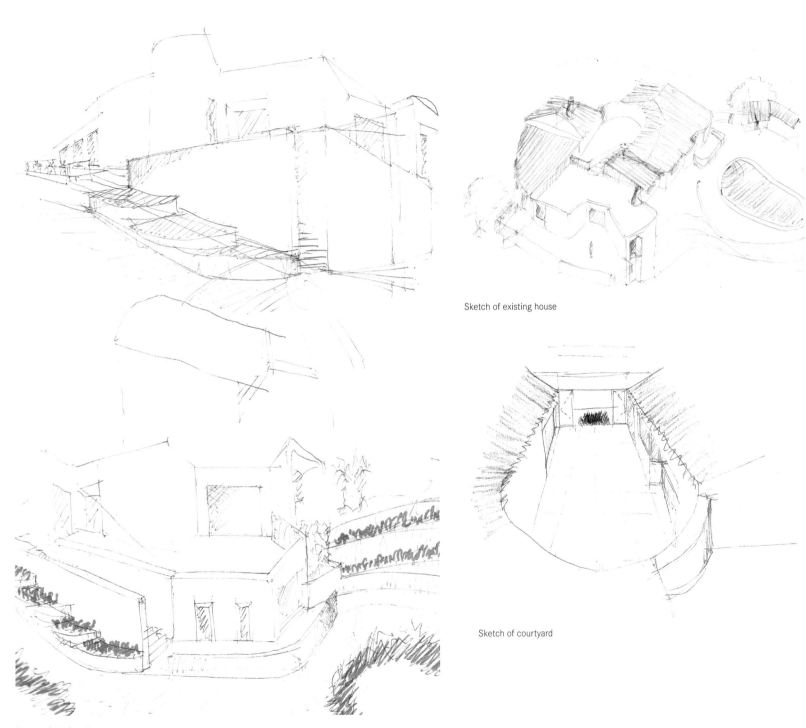

Sketch of existing house

Sketch of courtyard

Sketch of the façade

The pure white of all the walls in this house, interior and exterior, was restored with a rough-finished rustic plaster. Epoxy flooring was used in most of the rooms.

Le blanc pur de tous les murs de la maison, intérieurs et extérieurs, a été restauré avec du plâtre rustique (à finition rugueuse). Dans la majorité des pièces, de la résine époxy a été appliquée sur les sols.

Die reinweiße Farbe aller Wände des Hauses, innen und außen, wurde mit rustikalem Gips (mit rauem Finish) restauriert. Ein Epoxidgrund wurde auf den größten Teil der Aufenthaltsorte aufgetragen.

El color blanco puro de todas la paredes de la casa, interiores y exteriores, fue restaurado con yeso rústico (con acabado rugoso). Un suelo de epoxi se aplicó en la mayor parte de las estancias.

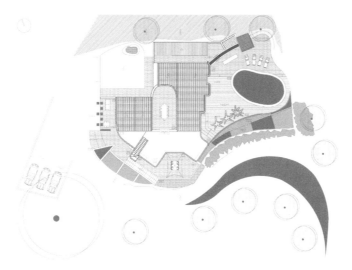

Roof plan

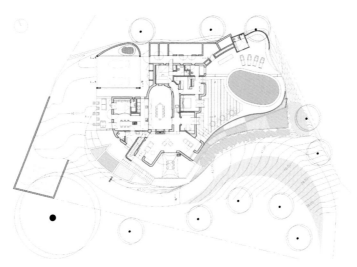

Ground floor plan

Lower floor plan (new flat)

Part of the kitchen furniture is finished in cement, which retains a rustic and informal feel more in keeping with a holiday house.

Une partie du mobilier de cuisine est réalisé avec des finitions en micro-ciment, ce qui permet de garder un aspect rustique et informel plus approprié à une maison de vacances.

Teile der Küchenausstattung wurden mit Mikrozement abgeschlossen, wodurch ein eher für Ferienhäuser typischer rustikaler und informaler Aspekt entsteht.

Parte del mobiliario de cocina está realizado con acabados de microcemento, lo cual permite mantener un aspecto rústico e informal más propio de una casa de vacaciones.

In the house, life is multidirectional and visually permeable within the different geographical directions permitted within this privileged environment.

Le mode de vie dans la maison est multidirectionnel et visuellement ouvert sur les différentes directions géographiques que permet son environnement privilégié.

In dem Wohnhaus ist das Lebensgefühl multidirektional und visuell durchlässig in die verschiedenen geografischen Richtungen, die seine privilegierte Umgebung zulässt.

En la vivienda, la experiencia de vida es multidireccional y visualmente permeable en las diferentes direcciones geográficas que su privilegiado entorno permite.

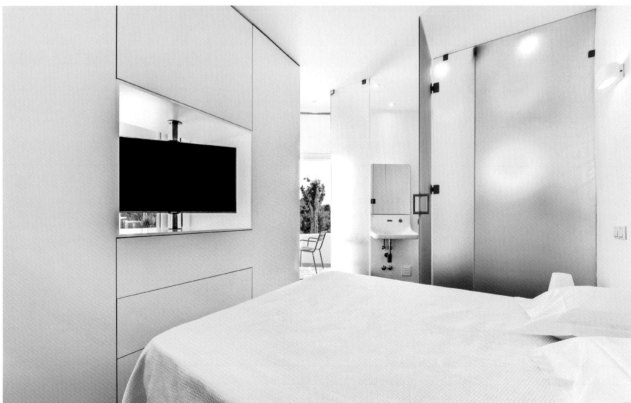

CENTENNIAL TREE HOUSE

Wallflower Architecture + Design
East Coast, Singapore
© Albert Lim

Introversion often has negative connotations. However, what for some is withdrawal and isolation is for others energy and ways to thrive in self-reflection and contemplation: life is inside. That is the basis upon which Wallflower Architecture + Design conceived this house, succeeding in creating a spacious interior in which to live that is completely isolated from its exterior environment.

Le repli sur soi a souvent des connotations négatives. Cependant, ce qui pour certains est synonyme de refuge et d'isolement, pour d'autres est synonyme d'énergie et une manière de s'épanouir dans l'autoréflexion et la contemplation : la vie est à l'intérieur. C'est de cette façon que Wallflower Architecture + Design conçoit la conception de la maison, et parvient à isoler complètement de l'environnement extérieur les larges parties communes.

Die Introversion ruft üblicherweise negative Konnotationen hervor. Dennoch bietet das, was für einige Rückzug und Isolation bedeutet, für andere Energie und Formen, in Selbstreflexion und Kontemplation zu schwelgen: Das Leben findet innen statt. So konzipiert Wallflower Architecture + Design den Entwurf des Wohnhauses und erreicht, dass es einem weiten Innenlebensraum gelingt, sich vollständig von der umgebenden Außenwelt abzugrenzen.

La introversión suele tener connotaciones negativas. Sin embargo, lo que para algunos es retiro y aislamiento, para otros es energía y formas de prosperar en la auto reflexión y la contemplación: la vida se encuentra dentro. Así es como Wallflower Architecture + Design concibe el diseño de la vivienda, y consigue que un amplio interior de vida logre aislarse por completo del exterior circundante.

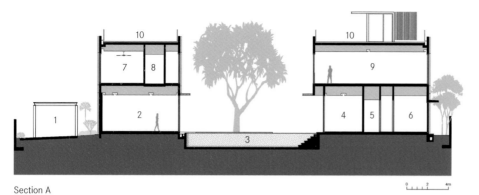

Section A

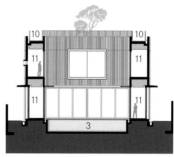

Section B

0 2 4m

1. Parking
2. Living room
3. Swimming pool
4. Kitchen
5. Powder room
6. Laundry
7. Bedroom
8. Bathroom
9. Master bedroom
10. Timber deck
11. Corridor

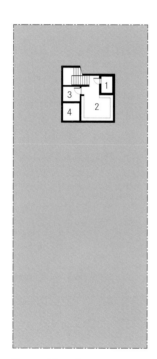

Basement floor plan

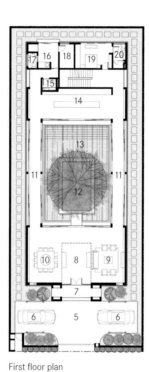

First floor plan

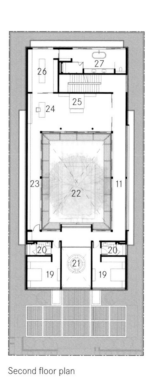

Second floor plan

Roof plan

0 2 4m

1. HS	11. Corridor	21. Void to foyer
2. Store room	12. Courtyard	22. Void to courtyard
3. Pump room	13. Swimming pool	23. Library
4. Balancing tank	14. Kitchen	24. Study
5. Driveway	15. Powder room	25. Master bedroom
6. Parking	16. Laundry	26. Walk-in wardrobe
7. Entrance porch	17. Toilet	27. Master bathroom
8. Foyer	18. Utility room	28. Planter
9. Living room	19. Bedroom	29. Timber deck
10. Dining room	20. Bathroom	30. Air-con

The wooden screens along the entire perimeter of the first floor allow the breeze to enter, naturally cooling the passageways and living spaces.

Les panneaux en bois sur tout le périmètre du premier étage permettent à la brise de s'engouffrer et de rafraîchir naturellement les couloirs et les parties communes.

Die Schutzwände aus Holz um das gesamte erste Stockwerk erlauben es, dass der Wind hindurchgeht und so auf natürliche Weise Gänge und Lebensräume erfrischt.

Las pantallas de madera a lo largo de todo el perímetro del primer piso permiten el paso de la brisa, y que refresque con naturalidad pasillos y espacios de vida.

MULTIPLE GENERATION HOUSE

franz
Eichgraben, Austria
© franz

In an era that is characterised by one-person households and single-parent families, this project by franz is an example of how three generations can live together in a contemporary architectural building. The project evolved from the renovation of an old house through to its expansion into a modern facility that houses a family that has grown from three to five members, including grandmother.

À une époque qui se caractérise par des foyers unipersonnels et des familles uni-parentales, le travail de franz est un exemple de la façon dont trois générations peuvent vivre ensemble dans une maison à l'architecture contemporaine. Le projet commence par la rénovation d'une ancienne maison et s'agrandit par une structure moderne accueillant une famille qui est passée de trois à cinq membres, dont la grand-mère.

In Zeiten, die sich durch Einpersonenhaushalte und Familien mit nur einem Elternteil auszeichnen, ist die Arbeit von franz ein Beispiel dafür, wie drei Generationen gemeinsam in einem Gebäude mit zeitgenössischer Architektur leben können. Das Projekt entwickelt sich von der Sanierung eines alten Hauses bis zu dessen Erweiterung in einem modernen Bau, das nun eine Familie beherbergt, die von drei auf fünf Mitglieder einschließlich Großmutter gewachsen ist.

En tiempos caracterizados por hogares unipersonales y familias uniparentales, el trabajo de franz es un ejemplo de cómo tres generaciones pueden vivir juntas en un edificio de arquitectura contemporánea. El proyecto evoluciona desde la renovación de una antigua casa, hasta su ampliación en una moderna estructura que acoge a una familia que ha crecido de tres a cinco integrantes, abuela incluida.

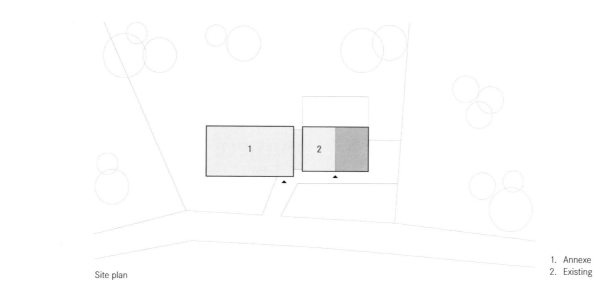

Site plan

1. Annexe
2. Existing

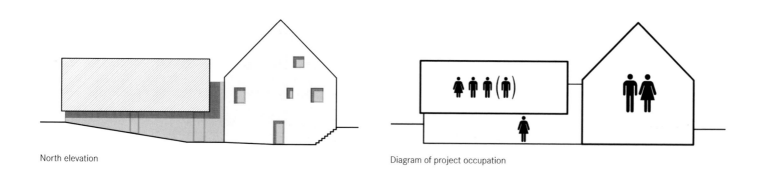

North elevation

Diagram of project occupation

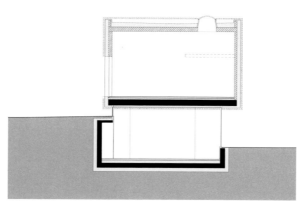

Section

Both the exterior of the large box, like the ground floor roof and the inner wall at the glass junction between the two buildings, are lined with solid larch.

L'extérieur du grand cube, ainsi que le plafond du rez-de-chaussée et le mur intérieur qui réunit par une verrière les deux bâtiments, sont revêtus de bois massif en mélèze.

Sowohl die Außenseite des großen Blocks als auch das Dach des Erdgeschosses und die Innenwand im Glasteil zwischen den beiden Gebäuden sind mit massivem Lärchenholz verschalt.

Tanto el exterior de la gran caja, como el techo de la planta baja y la pared interior en la unión de vidrio entre los dos edificios, están revestidos con madera maciza de alerce.

410

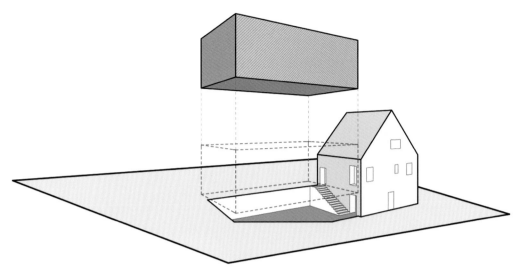

Diagram of new structure

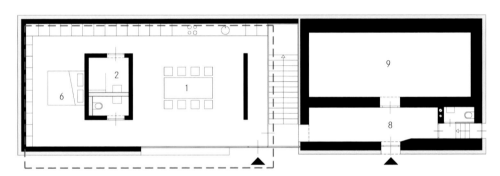

Ground floor plan

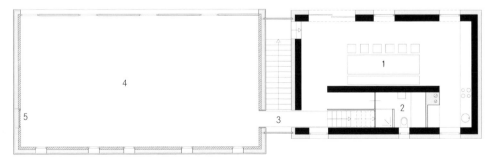

1. Living room
2. Bathroom
3. Runway
4. Children's room/
   Optional divisible
5. Optical access
6. Bedroom
7. Bathroom
8. Anteroom
9. Storage room

Basement floor plan

The large wooden box, which is currently a large games room for the children, is ready-prepared for future separation into four large individual rooms.

Le grand cube en bois, qui est maintenant une grande salle de jeu pour les enfants, est prêt à être divisé prochainement en quatre grandes pièces séparées.

Der große Holzblock, der jetzt ein riesiges Spielzimmer für die Kinder ist, wurde für seine spätere Teilung in vier große getrennte Zimmer vorbereitet.

La gran caja de madera, que ahora es una gran sala de juego para los niños, está preparada para su futura partición en cuatro grandes habitaciones separadas.

HOUSE IN CAMPS BAY

Luis Mira Architects
Cape Town, South Africa
© Luis Mira, © Wieland Gleich
www.archigraphy.com

The privileged location of the land and the generous Cape Town climate guided Luis Mira's design process with accuracy. The rooms frame the ocean views and the open spaces facing the mountains. Furthermore, although the house is conceived as a large, open studio, it can be transformed to create individual private spaces when friends visit.

La situation privilégiée du terrain et le climat généreux de la ville du Cap ont guidé précisément le processus de conception de Luis Mira : les pièces ont vue sur l'océan et les espaces ouverts regardent les montagnes. En outre, bien que la maison soit conçue comme un grand espace ouvert, elle est capable de se transformer et de créer des espaces privés et individuels lorsqu'il y a des visites.

Die privilegierte Lage des Grundstücks und das großzügige Klima von Ciudad del Cabo leiteten den Entwurfsprozess von Luis Mira präzise: Die Zimmer umrahmen die Aussicht auf den Ozean und von den offenen Räumen aus schaut man auf die Berge. Zudem kann sich das Wohnhaus, obwohl es wie ein großes offenes Studio wirkt, verwandeln und private und persönliche Räume entstehen lassen, wenn Besuch kommt.

La privilegiada situación del terreno y el clima generoso de Ciudad del Cabo guiaron el proceso de diseño de Luis Mira con precisión: las habitaciones enmarcan las vistas hacia el océano y los espacios abiertos miran a las montañas. Además, aunque la vivienda se concibe como un gran estudio abierto, es capaz de transformarse y crear espacios privados e individuales cuando acuden visitas.

The essential concept of luxury is found in the continuous expansion and opening up of the interior spaces to make the most of the unique and exquisite South African climate.

Le concept essentiel du luxe est l'élargissement et l'ouverture continue des espaces intérieurs pour profiter pleinement du climat sud-africain unique et agréable.

Das essentielle Konzept des Luxus ist die fortgesetzte Erweiterung und Öffnung der inneren Räume, um das einzigartige und exquisite südafrikanische Klima voll und ganz auszunutzen.

El concepto esencial del lujo es la continua ampliación y apertura de los espacios interiores para beneficiarse plenamente del único y exquisito clima sudafricano.

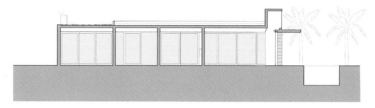

Section A-A

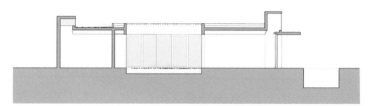

Section B-B

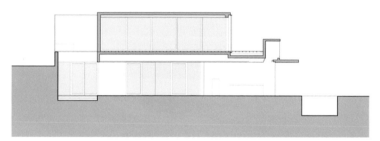

Section C-C

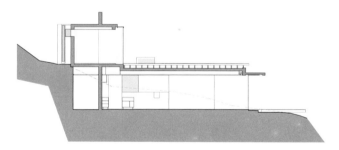

Section D-D

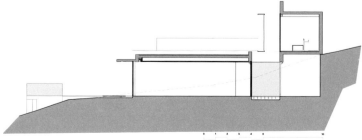

Section E-E

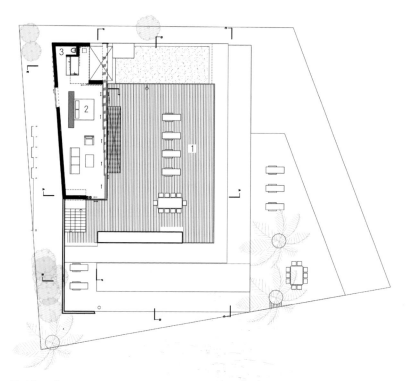

First floor plan

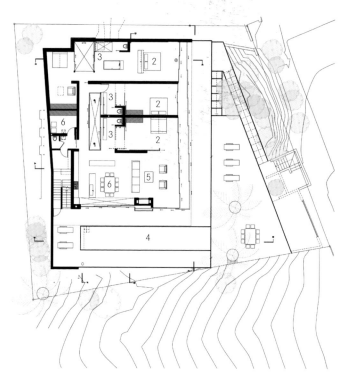

Ground floor plan

1. Terrace
2. Bedroom
3. Bathroom
4. Swimming pool
5. Living room
6. Kitchen/Dining room
7. Toilet

The use of neutral and natural materials reflects the desire to bring the outdoors inside, contrasting the lush surrounding terrain with the intense white interior.

L'utilisation de matériaux neutres et naturels reflète le désir d'amener l'extérieur à l'intérieur, et de confronter le terrain luxuriant avec le blanc intense de l'intérieur.

Die Verwendung neutraler und natürlicher Materialien entspringt dem Wunsch, das Außen nach innen mitzunehmen und der üppigen Umgebung durch das intensiv weiße Innere einen Kontrast entgegenzusetzen.

El uso de materiales neutros y naturales responde al deseo de llevar el exterior al interior, y contrastar el exuberante terreno circundante con el intenso blanco interior.

HOUSE VON STEIN

Philipp Architekten
Frankfurt, Germany
© Jose Campos

Philipp Architekten's project took place on a gently sloping corner of a growing residential area of Frankfurt. The design ensures that owners enjoy both maximum privacy and plenty of openness. The clients achieved their wish of creating a house in which they could enjoy a Los Angeles loft feel.

Le travail de Philipp Architekten a lieu dans le coin d'une rue légèrement en pente d'un quartier résidentiel de Francfort en pleine croissance. La conception permet aux propriétaires de bénéficier d'un maximum d'intimité, et en même temps, d'une grande ouverture sur l'extérieur. Les clients réalisent leur souhait de posséder une maison qui leur permet d'avoir la "sensation de *loft* à Los Angeles".

Die Arbeit von Philipp Architekten wird in einem Winkel eines sanften Hanges in einer Wohngegend Frankfurts realisiert, die derzeit boomt. Der Entwurf bietet den Eigentümern maximale Privatsphäre und gleichzeitig ein hohes Maß an Offenheit. Die Klienten sehen ihren Wunsch erfüllt, ein Wohnhaus zu besitzen, das sie das „Gefühl eines Lofts in Los Angeles" genießen lässt.

El trabajo de Philipp Architekten se lleva a cabo en una esquina de suave pendiente de una zona residencial de Frankfurt en pleno crecimiento. La diseño consigue que los propietarios gocen, al mismo tiempo, de máxima privacidad y de un alto grado de apertura. Los clientes ven cumplido su deseo de poseer una vivienda que les permite disfrutar de la "sensación de *loft* en Los Ángeles".

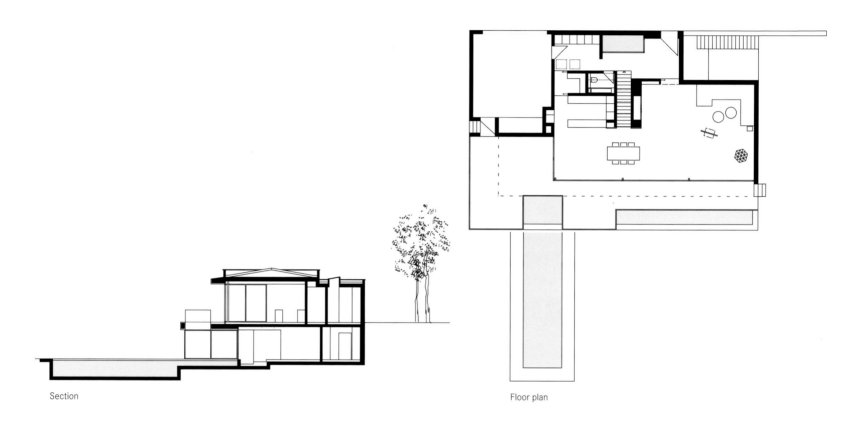

Section

Floor plan

The building is minimalist and only opens to the street via the front door and the garage. However, the section that faces the garden and pool is diaphanous and transparent.

Le bâtiment est minimaliste et s'ouvre sur la rue uniquement par la porte principale et le garage. Cependant, du côté de la partie orientée vers le jardin et la piscine il est translucide et transparent.

Das Gebäude ist minimalistisch und öffnet sich zur Straße nur über den Haupteingang und die Garage. Dennoch ist es auf der dem Garten und dem Pool zugewandten Seite durchsichtig und transparent.

El edificio es minimalista y solo se abre hacia la calle a través de la puerta principal y el garaje. Sin embargo, es diáfano y transparente en la parte orientada en dirección al jardín y la piscina.

Integrated on the ground floor, the pool is right next to the bedroom, making inside and outside intertwine through the ripples of light reflected on walls and ceilings.

La piscine, située au rez-de-chaussée, se trouve juste à côté de la chambre et est le trait d'union entre l'intérieur et l'extérieur grâce à la lumière ondulante qui se reflète sur les murs et les plafonds.

In die untere Ebene integriert befindet sich der Pool direkt neben dem Schlafzimmer und sorgt dafür, dass sich Innen und Außen durch die Wellenbewegung des sich auf Wänden und Dächern reflektierenden Lichts gegenseitig durchdringen.

Integrada en la planta baja, la piscina está justo al lado del dormitorio y hace que el interior y el exterior se entrelacen mediante la ondulación de la luz que se refleja en paredes y techos.

SAVA NAM

Original Vision
Natal Beach, Thailand
© Andrew Loiterton

The main focus of this house is on the first floor, where the living and dining spaces open seamlessly onto a large terrace and pool. Original Vision's design is a stylish beach house with a distinctive aesthetic and the latest gadgets. A spectacular project that uses the natural monsoon breezes to provide ventilation.

L'attention principale de la maison se porte sur le premier étage, où les parties communes et la salle à manger s'ouvrent à la perfection sur une large terrasse avec piscine. Le projet d'Original Vision est une maison de plage élégante avec une conception originale et des installations de dernière génération. Un projet spectaculaire qui utilise naturellement la brise de la mousson comme aération.

Der Hauptschwerpunkt dieses Wohnhauses liegt auf dem ersten Stock, wo sich Wohn- und Esszimmer perfekt zu einer großen Terrasse mit Pool öffnen. Das Projekt von Original Vision ist ein elegantes Strandhaus mit unverwechselbarem Design und Ausstattung der jüngsten Generation. Ein spektakuläres Projekt, das auf natürliche Weise die Passatwinde zur Ventilation nutzt.

El foco principal de atención de la vivienda se concentra en el primer piso, donde los espacios de estar y comedor se abren a la perfección a una amplia terraza con piscina. El proyecto de Original Vision es una elegante casa de playa con un diseño distintivo e instalaciones de última generación. Un proyecto espectacular que aprovecha de forma natural las brisas del monzón para ventilarse.

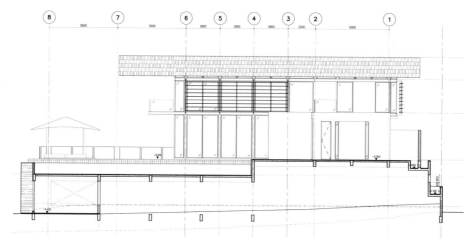

South elevation

West elevation

Section BB

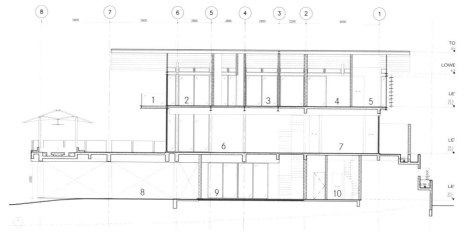

Section AA

1. Balcony
2. Master bedroom
3. Master ensuite
4. Bedroom
5. Study
6. Living room
7. Kitchen
8. Carport
9. Family room
10. Utility/Store room
11. Dining room
12. Wine cellar
13. Maid room

Access to all areas of the house, be it inward or outward, is via the first floor. This creates a dynamic and contemporary holiday home that is removed from urban life.

L'accès à toutes les parties de la maison, que ce soit à l'intérieur comme à l'extérieur, se fait par le premier étage. Cela donne ainsi une maison de vacances dynamique et contemporaine, isolée de la vie urbaine.

Der Zugang zu allen Bereichen der Villa, innen und außen, verläuft über den ersten Stock. Dadurch entsteht ein dynamisches zeitgenössisches Ferienhaus, das sich vom Leben in der Stadt deutlich unterscheidet.

El acceso a todas las áreas de la villa, ya sea hacia adentro o hacia afuera, es a través del primer piso. Se crea así un dinámica casa de vacaciones contemporánea y apartada de la vida urbana.

First floor plan

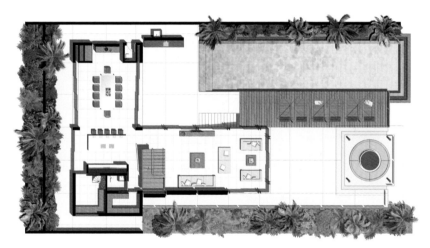

Ground floor plan

Basement floor plan

The open staircase of glass, steel and wood connects the three levels and helps to increase the feeling of space within the house.

L'escalier ouvert en verre, acier et bois relie les trois niveaux et permet d'amplifier la sensation d'espace dans la maison.

Die offene Treppe aus Glas, Stahl und Holz verbindet die drei Ebenen und trägt dazu bei, das Gefühl der Größe des Hauses noch zu verstärken.

La escalera abierta de cristal, acero y madera conecta los tres niveles y ayuda a aumentar la sensación de amplitud de la vivienda.

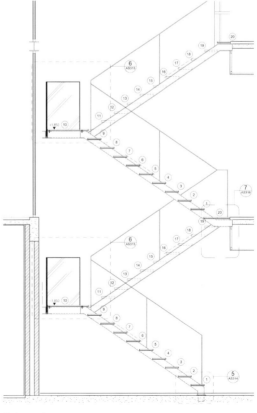

Stairs section

SILVER BAY

SAOTA - Stefan Antoni Olmesdahl Truen Architects
Shelley Point, South Africa
© SAOTA

The house's design fulfils three conditions imposed by its context: the first was to place the living spaces on the upper level to maximise views of the bay; the second was to avoid the wind from the southeast; and the third was to position the pool in a courtyard where it would capture the sun on the north side of the house. A wind-free open-air space to be enjoyed all year round.

La conception de la maison obéit à trois conditions contextuelles. Tout d'abord, la mise en place des parties communes à l'étage supérieur pour optimiser la vue sur la baie. Ensuite, éviter le vent prédominant du sud-est. Et pour finir, positionner la piscine sur une terrasse où le soleil donne du côté nord de la maison dans un espace extérieur mais sans vent pour profiter du soleil toute l'année.

Der Entwurf dieses Wohnhauses erfüllt drei kontextuelle Bedingungen. Erstens: Die Unterbringung der Lebensräume im oberen Stockwerk, um den Blick auf die Bucht maximal auszunutzen. Zweitens: Den überwiegend aus Südost wehenden Wind zu vermeiden. Und drittens: Den Pool in einem Patio anzulegen, wo er die Sonne auf der Nordseite des Hauses einfängt, ein Raum an der frischen Luft aber ohne Wind, der das ganze Jahr lang genossen werden kann.

El diseño de la vivienda cumple tres condiciones contextuales. La primera, la colocación de los espacios de vida en el nivel superior para maximizar las vistas de la bahía. La segunda, evitar el predominante viento del sudeste. Y la tercera, posicionar la piscina en un patio donde capturar el sol del lado norte de la casa, un espacio al aire libre pero sin viento para disfrutarlo todo el año.

Shelley Point, where this house is set, is a small spur of land that juts out into the Atlantic and is surrounded by beaches to the east, north and west.

Shelley Point, lieu où se trouve la maison, est une petite jetée qui s'avance dans l'Atlantique et est entourée de plages sur les flancs est, nord et ouest.

Shelley Point, wo sich dieses Haus befindet, ist eine kleine Landzunge, die in den Atlantik ragt und im Osten, Norden und Westen von Stränden umgeben ist.

Shelley Point, lugar en el que asienta la vivienda, es un pequeño espolón de tierra que se adentra en el Atlántico y rodeado de playas en los costados este, norte y oeste.

West elevation

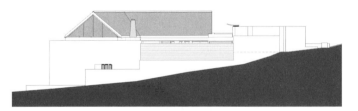

North elevation

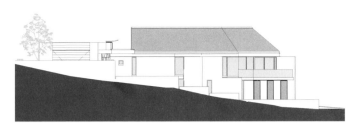

South elevation

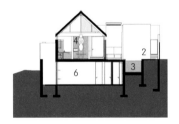

Section A-A

Section B-B

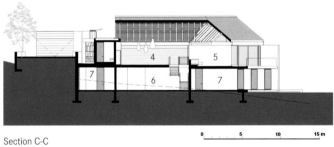

Section C-C

1. Parking
2. Deck
3. Swimming pool
4. Kitchen
5. Living/Dining room
6. Playroom
7. Bedroom
8. Main ensuite
9. Laundry

442

The top floor has been created as a single space containing the pool terrace, a raised entrance hall, a kitchen with a large table, a dining area and living room.

L'étage supérieur a été conçu comme un espace unique comprenant la terrasse de la piscine, un hall d'entrée surélevé, une cuisine avec une grande table, une salle à manger et un salon.

Das obere Stockwerk wurde als ein einziger Raum konzipiert, der den Pool im Außenbereich, eine erhöhte Eingangshalle, eine Küche mit großem Tisch und ein Wohn- und Esszimmer umfasst.

La planta superior se ha conceptualizado como un espacio único que contiene el patio de la piscina, un hall de entrada elevado, una cocina con una gran mesa y un comedor y sala de estar.

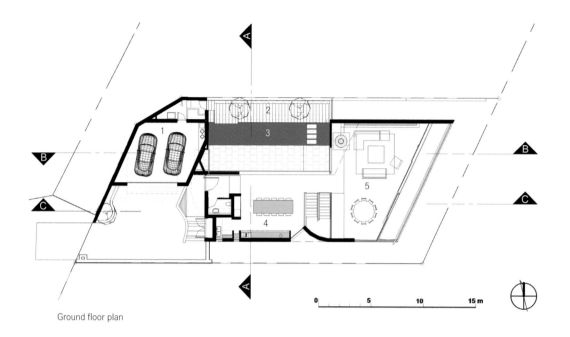

Ground floor plan

0   5   10   15 m

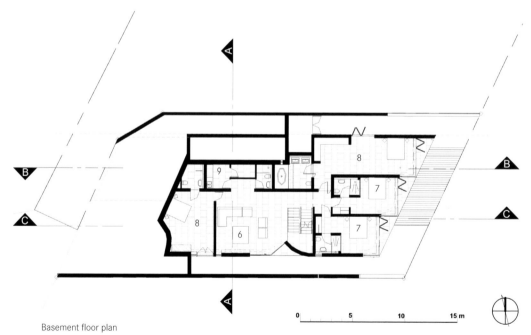

Basement floor plan

0   5   10   15 m

1. Parking
2. Deck
3. Swimming pool
4. Kitchen
5. Living/Dining room
6. Playroom
7. Bedroom
8. Main ensuite
9. Laundry

The simple cellular bedrooms have a serrated façade from which the completely glazed corners maximise the views.

Les chambres cellulaires simples ont une façade dentelée dont les extrémités entièrement vitrées permettent d'optimiser la vue.

Die einfachen zellulären Schlafzimmer verfügen über eine gezahnte Fassade, deren vollständige Verglasung der Ecken maximale Ausblicke ermöglicht.

Los dormitorios celulares simples tienen una fachada dentada donde el acristalamiento total de las esquinas permite maximizar las vistas.

SUN CAP HOUSE

Wallflower Architecture + Design
Sentosa Cove, Singapore
© Albert Lim

This Wallflower Architecture + Design project is set in a tropical environment with intense and powerful sunlight, but thanks to the proximity of the ocean it is blessed with a pleasant breeze, which is channelled through exclusive watercourses. In response to the urban density, the façade is a thick, nine-metre-high wall, which opens up to the views only at the rear.

El projet de Wallflower Architecture + Design est situé dans un environnement tropical dans lequel la lumière du soleil est forte et intense, mais où la proximité de l'océan la rend plus douce grâce à une agréable brise canalisée par des cours d'eau exclusifs. Face à la densité urbaine, la façade est un mur épais de neuf mètres de haut qui n'offre des vues que de la partie arrière.

Das Projekt von Wallflower Architecture + Design ist in einer tropischen Umgebung angesiedelt, in der das Sonnenlicht stark und intensiv ist, das jedoch durch die Nähe zum Ozean mit einer angenehmen Brise gesegnet ist, die durch die exklusiven Wasserläufe kanalisiert wird. Als Antwort auf die urbane Siedlungsdichte ist die Fassade eine grobe Mauer von neun Metern Höhe, die sich den Blicken nur im hinteren Teil öffnet.

El proyecto de Wallflower Architecture + Design se asienta en un entorno tropical en el que luz del sol es dura e intensa, pero donde la proximidad del océano lo bendice con una agradable brisa que se canaliza a través de los exclusivos cursos de agua. En respuesta a la densidad urbana, la fachada es un grueso muro de nueve metros de alto que solo se abre a las vistas en la parte posterior.

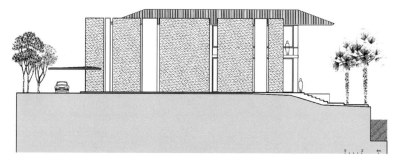

Elevation

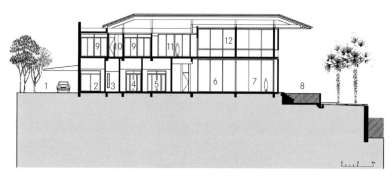

Section

First floor plan

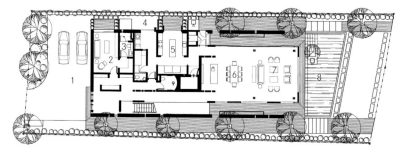

Second floor plan

1. Parking	8. Swimming pool
2. Guest room	9. Bedroom
3. Guest bathroom	10. Bathroom
4. Patio	11. Study
5. Kitchen	12. Master bedroom
6. Dining room	13. Master bathroom
7. Living room	

At the rear, a high glass structure surrounds the interior space. This also serves as a projector for views of the pool, garden and, further away, the water channels.

À l'arrière de la maison, une haute structure en verre entoure l'espace intérieur; elle permet en même temps d'avoir une vue sur la piscine et le jardin et, plus loin, sur les cours d'eau.

Im hinteren Teil umgibt eine hohe Glaskonstruktion den Innenraum, die zugleich den Blick auf das Schwimmbecken und den Garten und weiter hinten auf die Wasserläufe ermöglicht.

En la parte posterior, una alta estructura de vidrio envuelve el espacio interior; al mismo tiempo, permite proyectar las vistas hacia la piscina y el jardín y, más allá, hacia los cursos de agua.

The entrance and sidewalls mainly serve to provide privacy and filter the heat. They prevent the neighbours from seeing in whilst drawing the breeze through the house and not around its exterior.

Les murs de l'entrée et ceux sur les côtés servent essentiellement de filtre thermique et à préserver l'intimité. Ils permettent d'empêcher le regard des voisins mais laissent entrer la brise dans la maison et non autour de celle-ci.

Die Wände des Einganges und die Seitenwände sind im Wesentlichen ein Wärmefilter und sorgen für Privatsphäre. Zum einen verhindern sie die Blicke der Nachbarn, zum anderen lenken sie die frische Brise am Haus entlang statt in die Umgebung.

Las paredes de la entrada y los laterales son esencialmente un filtro térmico y de privacidad. Estas impiden las miradas de los vecinos pero permiten el paso de la brisa a través de la casa y no a su alrededor.

The parallel walls are not joined to the roof eaves. A one-metre gap breaks the distinction between inside and out, and invites the sun and light to bathe the vegetation growing on both sides of the wall.

Les murs parallèles ne s'unissent pas avec les auvents du toit. Une brèche d'un mètre efface la séparation entre l'intérieur et l'extérieur, et invite la lumière du soleil à baigner la végétation qui pousse de chaque côté du mur.

Die parallelen Wände verschmelzen nicht mit der Traufe des Daches. Eine Spalte von einem Meter hebt die Trennung von Innen und Außen auf und lädt das Sonnenlicht ein, sich über die auf beiden Seiten der Mauer wachsende Vegetation zu ergießen.

Las paredes paralelas no se unen con los aleros del techo. Una brecha de un metro borra la distinción interior-exterior, e invita a la luz del sol a bañar la vegetación que crece en ambos lados del muro.

THE W.I.N.D. HOUSE

UNStudio
Noord-Holland, The Netherlands
© Inga Powilleit, © Fedde de Weert

Major sustainability and automation solutions are integrated within UNStudio's original home. However, the design of this contemporary house does not rest solely on these aspects. The great flexibility of the spaces, the complete assimilation of the surrounding landscape and the centrifugal air flow form the basis of this smart home.

La maison originale d'UNStudio propose de grandes solutions de durabilité et d'automatisation. Cependant, la conception de cette maison contemporaine ne se centre pas uniquement sur ces aspects. La grande flexibilité des espaces, l'intégration complète du paysage environnant et la circulation centrifuge forment la base de la conception de cette maison intelligente.

Das originelle Haus von UNStudio integriert große Nachhaltigkeits- und Automatisierungslösungen. Dennoch konzentriert sich das Design dieses zeitgemäßen Hauses nicht nur auf diese Aspekte. Die hohe Flexibilität der Räume, die vollständige Assimilation der umgebenden Landschaft und die Zentrifugallüftung bilden die Basis des Entwurfes dieses intelligenten Hauses.

La original vivienda de UNStudio integra grandes soluciones de sostenibilidad y de automatización. Sin embargo, el diseño de esta vivienda contemporánea no solo se centra en estos aspectos para completar su diseño. La gran flexibilidad de los espacios, la asimilación completa del paisaje circundante y la circulación centrífuga forman la base del diseño de esta vivienda inteligente.

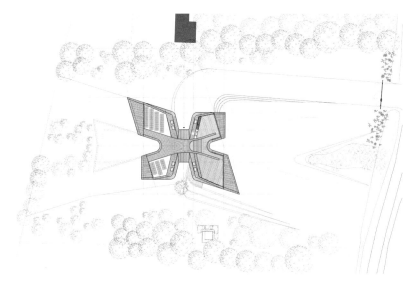

Site plan

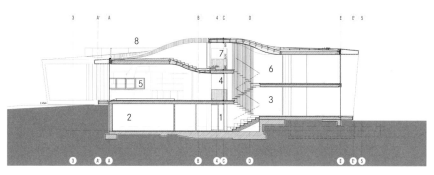

Section

1. Hall- Entrance level
2. Basement/Storage
3. Gallery – Level children/Music room
4. Hall – Level Living/Dining
5. Kitchen/Dining
6. Gallery – Level Master bedroom
7. Hall – Level access roof terrace
8. Roof terrace

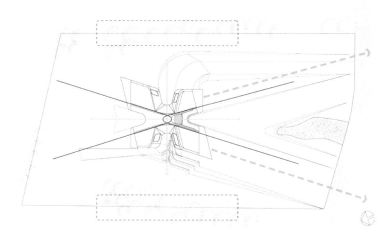

Vistas diagram

Light orientation diagram

Wind and vistas orientation diagram

464

The walls and ceilings are covered with natural clay plaster. The main walls are made of clay bricks, helping to ensure a healthy indoor climate.

Les murs et les plafonds de la maison sont recouverts d'un stuc d'argile naturel. Les murs principaux sont en briques d'argile et permettent que l'ambiance intérieure soit meilleure pour la santé.

Wände und Decken des Hauses sind mit natürlichem Ton verputzt. Die Hauptwände sind aus Tonziegeln und tragen zu einem gesunden Raumklima bei.

Las paredes y los techos de la casa están revestidos con un estuco de arcilla natural. Las paredes principales son de ladrillos de arcilla y ayudan a que el clima interior sea saludable.

The main shape of the house
evokes the form of a simple
flower. The four façades that curve
towards the interior create four
wings, like petals, which draw the
landscape inside.

Der Grundriss erinnert an die Form
einer einfachen Blume. Die vier
nach innen kurvigen Fassaden
bilden vier Blütenblättern ähnliche
Flügel, die die Landschaft im
Inneren zeichnen.

Le plan principal de la maison
suggère la forme d'une simple
fleur. Les quatre façades arrondies
vers l'intérieur forment quatre
ailes, comme des pétales, qui
dessinent le paysage à l'intérieur.

El plano principal de la vivienda
sugiere la forma de una sencilla
flor. Las cuatro fachadas curvadas
hacia el interior crean cuatro alas,
como pétalos, que dibujan el
paisaje en el interior.

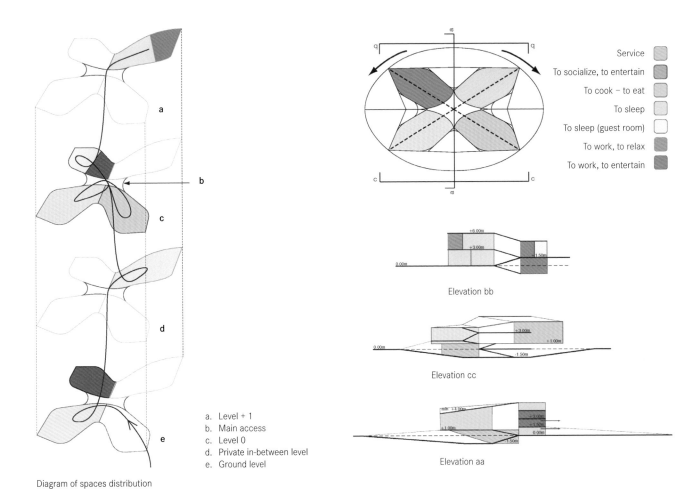

Service
To socialize, to entertain
To cook – to eat
To sleep
To sleep (guest room)
To work, to relax
To work, to entertain

a. Level + 1
b. Main access
c. Level 0
d. Private in-between level
e. Ground level

Diagram of spaces distribution

+6.00m
+3.00m
0.00m
+1.50m

Elevation bb

+3.00m
0.00m
+1.00m
-1.50m

Elevation cc

min +4.00m
+1.00m
+3.00m
+1.50m
0.00m
-1.50m

Elevation aa

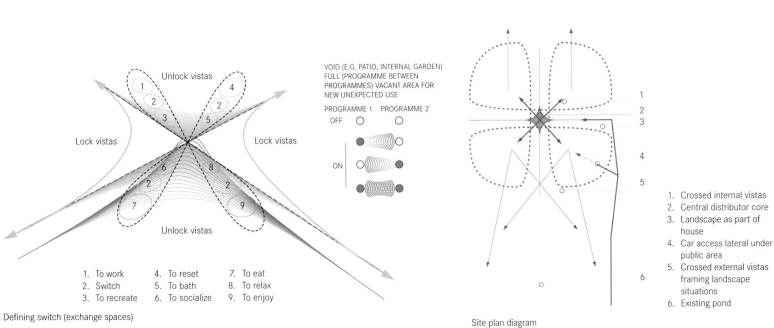

Unlock vistas

Lock vistas   Lock vistas

Unlock vistas

1. To work   4. To reset   7. To eat
2. Switch   5. To bath   8. To relax
3. To recreate 6. To socialize 9. To enjoy

Defining switch (exchange spaces)

VOID (E.G. PATIO, INTERNAL GARDEN)
FULL (PROGRAMME BETWEEN
PROGRAMMES) VACANT AREA FOR
NEW UNEXPECTED USE

PROGRAMME 1   PROGRAMME 2
OFF   ○   ○

ON

1. Crossed internal vistas
2. Central distributor core
3. Landscape as part of
   house
4. Car access lateral under
   public area
5. Crossed external vistas
   framing landscape
   situations
6. Existing pond

Site plan diagram

467

TRAVERTINE DREAM HOUSE

Wallflower Architecture + Design
Serangoon, Singapore
© Jeremy San

This Wallflower Architecture + Design project meets its clients' simple needs of functionality, maximising the property's usable space and incorporating vegetation. Aesthetically, the requirement was to use travertine extensively as an architectural finish. Thus the house is inspired by the Italian landscape so often visited by its owners.

Le projet de Wallflower Architecture + Design satisfait les désirs simples de ses clients. Fonctionnellement, ils doivent optimiser la superficie utile de la maison et intégrer de la végétation. Esthétiquement, ils doivent largement utiliser du travertin comme finition architecturale. Par conséquent, la maison s'inspire du paysage urbain italien que les propriétaires ont visité à de nombreuses occasions.

Dieses Projekt von Wallflower Architecture + Design befriedigt die einfachen Wünsche seiner Eigentümer. Funktional sollte die Wohnfläche vergrößert und Vegetation einbezogen werden. Ästhetisch sollte der Travertin in großem Umfang als architektonischer Abschluss zum Einsatz kommen. So ist das Haus durch die urbane Landschaft Italiens inspiriert, die seine Eigentümer so oft besucht haben.

El proyecto de Wallflower Architecture + Design satisface los sencillos deseos de sus clientes. Funcionalmente, maximizar la superficie útil de la vivienda e incorporar vegetación. Estéticamente, utilizar el travertino extensamente como acabado arquitectónico. Por tanto, la vivienda se inspira en el paisaje urbano italiano tantas veces visitado por sus propietarios.

The house is set out as two parallel blocks connected by an enclosed glass bridge. The separation between the two blocks allows light into the basement spaces.

La maison est formée de deux blocs parallèles reliés par un pont en verre fermé. La séparation entre les deux blocs permet à la lumière d'être transmise aux espaces du sous-sol.

Das Haus besteht aus zwei parallelen Blocks, die durch eine geschlossene Glasbrücke verbunden sind. Der Abstand zwischen den beiden Blocks erlaubt es, dass Licht bis in die Räume im Untergeschoss gelangt.

La casa se organiza en dos bloques paralelos conectados por un puente de cristal cerrado. La separación entre los dos bloques permite que la luz se transmita a los espacios del sótano.

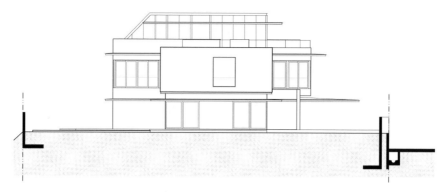

Side elevation

Front elevation

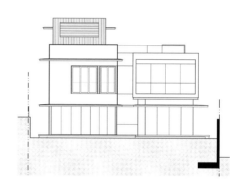

Rear elevation

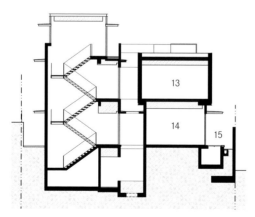

Section A

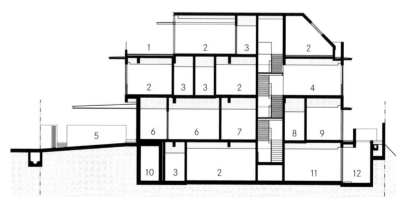

Section B

1. Roof timber deck
2. Bedroom
3. Bathroom
4. Family room
5. Parking
6. Kitchen
7. Patio
8. Guest bathroom
9. Guest bedroom
10. HS
11. Maid room
12. Garden
13. Master bedroom
14. Living room
15. Outdoor deck

To incorporate as many green and 'blue' spaces as possible, gardens and water features are scattered all over the house.

Pour accueillir autant d'espaces verts et "bleus" que possible, les jardins et les plans d'eau sont répartis dans toute la maison.

Um möglichst viele grüne und „blaue" Räume unterzubringen, verteilen sich die Gärten und Wasserelemente über das gesamte Haus.

Para dar cabida a la mayor cantidad de espacios verdes y "azules" como sea posible, los jardines y los cuerpos de agua se reparten por toda la casa.

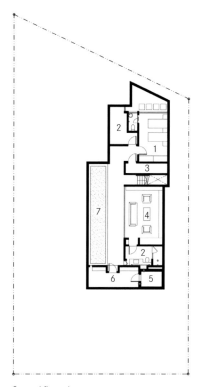

Second floor plan

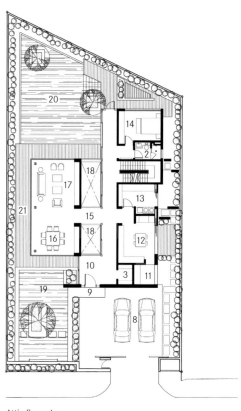

Attic floor plan

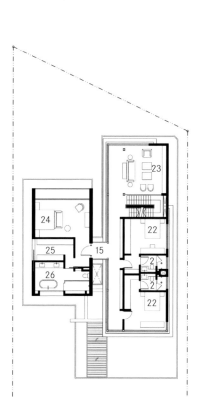

Basement plan

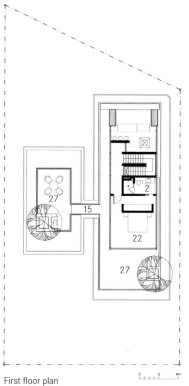

First floor plan

1. Maid's room
2. Bathroom
3. Store room
4. Entertainment room
5. HS
6. Mechanical room
7. Garden
8. Parking
9. Entrance
10. Foyer
11. Wet kitchen
12. Dry kitchen
13. Patio
14. Guest room
15. Link way
16. Dining room
17. Living room
18. Void to basement
19. Pond
20. Swimming pool
21. Outdoor deck
22. Bedroom
23. Family room
24. Master bedroom
25. Wardrobe
26. Master bathroom
27. Roof terrace

HOUSE FOR JULIA AND BJÖRN

Innauer-Matt Architekten ZT GMBH
Egg, Austria
© Adolf Bereuter

Clamped between a lemon tree and a walnut tree, the new house comfortably completes the small village in which it is located. Due to the incline and the narrowness of the plot on which it sits, the clear lines of the Innauer-Matt Architekten designed building follows the contours and makes use of the sloping land.

La nouvelle maison, située entre un citronnier et un noyer, complète joliment le petit hameau où elle se trouve. En raison de l'inclinaison et de la nature étroite du terrain où elle se trouve, la stratification du bâtiment clairement conçue par Innauer-Matt Architekten suit le contour et fait usage du terrain en pente.

Das neue Haus, zwischen einem Zitronen- und einem Nussbaum, ergänzt auf angenehme Weise den kleinen Hof, auf dem es sich befindet. Aufgrund der Neigung und der dichten Natur des Grundstücks, auf dem es liegt, folgt die klare Stratifikation des von Innauer-Matt Architekten entworfenen Gebäudes den Linien der Umgebung und nutzt die Hanglage aus.

La nueva vivienda, sujeta entre un limonero y un nogal, completa cómodamente el pequeño caserío en el que se encuentra. Debido a la inclinación y la naturaleza estrecha del terreno en el que se asienta, la clara estratificación del edificio diseñado por Innauer-Matt Architekten sigue las líneas de contorno y hace uso de la tierra en pendiente.

The entrance is on the first floor and a staircase leads to the ground floor, guided by the lateral light. Here, the entire space is taken up by a single living area—kitchen, dining room and lounge.

L'entrée se trouve au premier étage et, guidée par la lumière qui entre sur le côté, un escalier mène au rez-de-chaussée. Ici, le salon occupe tout l'espace pour manger, cuisiner et vivre.

Der Eingang befindet sich im ersten Stock und geleitet durch den Eintritt von Seitenlicht führt eine Treppe in das untere Geschoss. Hier beansprucht der Wohnraum den gesamten Raum — essen, kochen und wohnen.

La entrada se encuentra en el primer piso y, guiada por la entrada de luz lateral, una escalera conduce a la planta baja. Aquí, la sala de estar ocupa todo el espacio —comer, cocinar y vivir.

A large window with window
seat offers a spectacular view
of the village below and the
mountain scenery.

Une grande fenêtre avec un banc
offre une vue spectaculaire sur le
village qui se trouve en contrebas
ainsi que sur les montagnes.

Ein großes Fenster mit einer Bank
bietet einen spektakulären Blick
auf das weiter unten liegende Dorf
und die Berglandschaft.

Una ventana de gran tamaño
con un banco ofrece una vista
espectacular de la aldea que
se encuentra más abajo y del
paisaje montañoso.

All the furniture and floors are made of solid pine from the nearby forests. These are alternated with hand-made plaster surfaces and grey marble powder produced on site.

Tous les meubles et les sols sont en bois de sapin massif provenant des forêts avoisinantes, et alternent avec des surfaces en plâtre faîtes à la main et de la poudre de marbre gris clair produite sur place.

Alle Möbel und Böden bestehen aus massivem Tannenholz aus den nahe gelegenen Wäldern; sie wechseln sich mit handgearbeiteten Flächen aus Gips und vor Ort produziertem hellgrauen Marmorstaub ab.

Todos los muebles y suelos son de madera maciza de abeto de los bosques cercanos; se alternan con superficies de yeso hechas a mano y de polvo de mármol gris claro producido en el lugar.

AFSHARIAN'S HOUSE

ReNa Design (Reza Najafian)
Kermanshah, Iran
© Reza Najafian, © Mohamad Hosein Hamzehlouei

This client wanted to create a house that could be separated in the future for his two children, so ReNa Design's project came from the perspective of transforming the house into apartments. The client's other requirement was to create a unique exterior, which is achieved by making the house into a giant cube with a central crack, a building converted into a sculpture that rises from the street.

Pour que le client puisse offrir, dans l'avenir, à ses deux enfants, une maison séparée à chacun d'eux, le but du projet de ReNa Design est de pouvoir transformer la maison en appartements. L'autre demande du client est d'avoir un design extérieur unique. La maison est donc conçue comme un cube avec une grande fissure centrale. Un bâtiment devenu sculpture qui émerge de la rue.

Damit der Eigentümer seinen zwei Kindern in Zukunft eine eigene separate Wohnung bieten kann, wurde der Entwurf von ReNa Design mit der Perspektive entwickelt, das Haus in Apartments umzuwandeln. Die andere Vorgabe des Eigentümers, ein einzigartiges Außendesign, wird durch die Schaffung eines Würfels mit einer großen Spalte in der Mitte erreicht: Ein Gebäude, das in eine sich aus der Straße erhebende Skulptur verwandelt wurde.

Para que el cliente pudiese proporcionar a sus dos hijos una vivienda propia y separada en el futuro, el diseño de ReNa Design se desarrolla con la perspectiva de conseguir transformar la casa en apartamentos. La otra demanda del cliente, un diseño exterior único, se consigue haciendo de la vivienda un cubo con una gran grieta central, un edificio convertido en una escultura que surge de la calle.

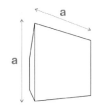

Process diagram

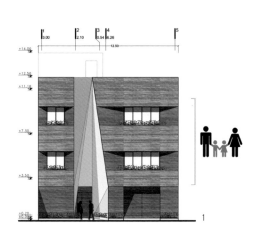

1

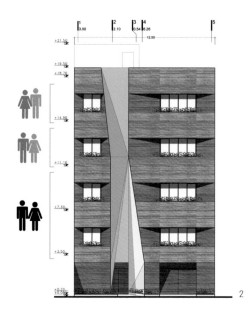

2

1

2

North elevation

1. Today's house
2. Tomorrow's apartment

The large crack in the main façade opens up the entrance clearly while also providing a comfortable response to the spatial divisions of the upper levels.

La grande fissure dans la façade principale est clairement l'entrée, mais elle répond également aux divisions de l'espace des niveaux supérieurs de manière commode.

Der tiefe Spalt in der Hauptfassade öffnet den Eingang auf klare Weise, reagiert aber auch auf angenehme Art auf die räumlichen Trennungen der oberen Stockwerke.

La gran grieta en la fachada principal abre la entrada de forma clara, pero también responde a las divisiones espaciales de los niveles superiores de una forma cómoda.

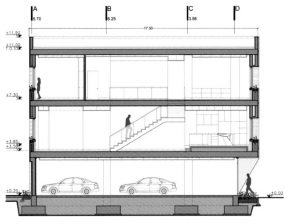

Section A-A

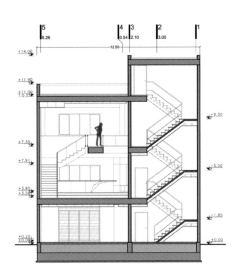

Section B-B

Section C-C

Respect for pedestrians is a beautiful concept in Iranian traditions, which is incorporated unashamedly in this project by inclining the ground-floor façade slightly backwards.

Le respect pour les passants, un beau concept dans les traditions iraniennes, apparait sans complexes dans ce projet en inclinant légèrement la façade en arrière au rez-de-chaussée.

Der Respekt für die Passanten, ein wunderschönes Konzept in den iranischen Traditionen, zeigt sich ohne Zweifel in diesem Projekt, indem die Fassade im Erdgeschoss leicht nach hinten geneigt ist.

El respeto a los transeúntes, un concepto precioso en las tradiciones iraníes, emerge sin complejos en este proyecto al inclinarse la fachada ligeramente hacia atrás en la planta baja.

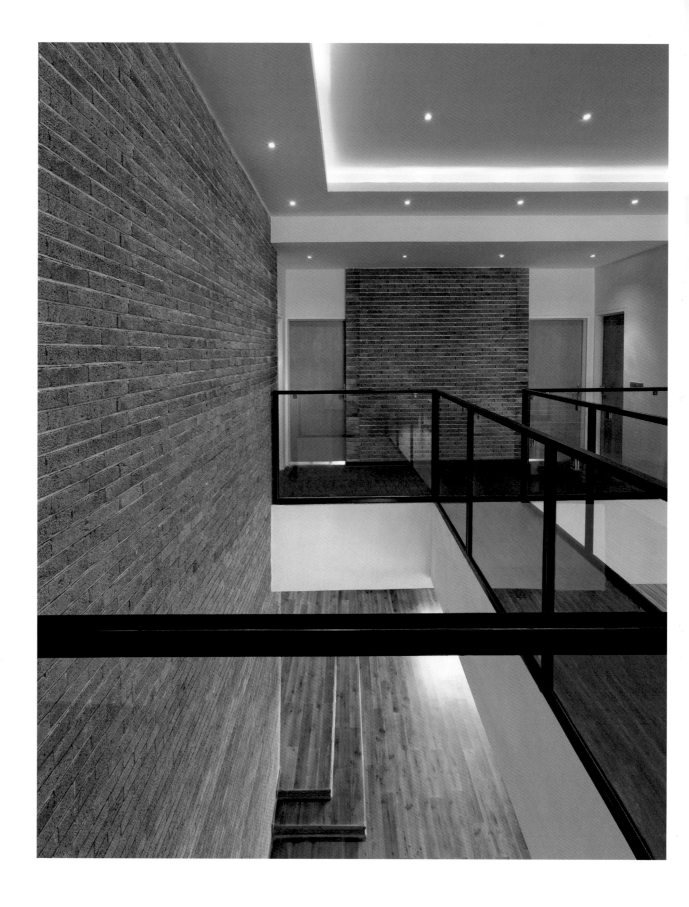

Second floor plan

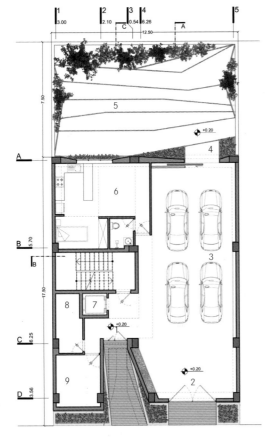

Basement floor plan

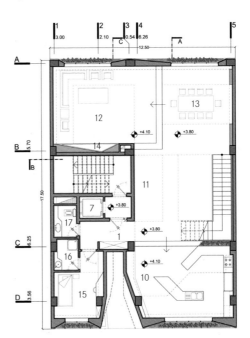

First floor plan

1. Entrance
2. Parking entrance
3. Parking
4. Patio entrance
5. Patio
6. Studio apartment
7. Elevator
8. Storage room
9. Mechanical room
10. Kitchen
11. Living room
12. Drawing room
13. Dining room
14. Fireplace
15. Guest bedroom
16. Bathroom
17. Toilet
18. Bedroom
19. Master bedroom
20. Void